YOUR FAVOURITES

ALL PLANTS

BISH BASH
BOSH!

HENRY FIRTH & IAN THEASBY

This book is dedicated to you.
Thanks for picking it up.
We hope you love it.

HQ
An imprint of HarperCollins*Publishers* Ltd
1 London Bridge Street
London SE1 9GF

10 9 8 7 6 5 4 3 2 1

First published in Great Britain by HQ
An imprint of HarperCollins*Publishers* Ltd 2019

Text Copyright © Henry Firth and Ian Theasby 2019

Design and Photography Copyright © HQ, an imprint
of HarperCollins*Publishers* Ltd 2019

Henry Firth and Ian Theasby assert the moral right to be identified as
the authors of this work. A catalogue record for this book is available
from the British Library.

ISBN 978-0-00-832705-7

Our policy is to use papers that are natural, renewable and
recyclable products and made from wood grown in sustainable
forests. The logging and manufacturing processes conform to
the legal environmental regulations of the country of origin.

For more information visit: www.harpercollins.co.uk/green

Photography: Lizzie Mayson
Food styling: Frankie Unsworth
Prop styling: Sarah Birks
Design: Paul Palmer-Edwards
Creative Director: Louise McGrory
Editorial Director: Rachel Kenny
Senior Commissioning Editor: Kate Fox
Project Editor: Laura Herring
Production Controller: Stefanie Kruszyk

Printed and bound in Italy by Rotolito S.p.A.

Contents

Welcome

Your favourite food. All plants. Sorted.

Whether you're after a quick mid-week meal, you need to satisfy those comfort food cravings, or maybe it's the weekend and you want to cook a full roast dinner to impress the in-laws, we have all your favourite recipes covered. We even have the solution for when only the most decadent chocolate cake will do . . .

Whatever your go-to, all-time favourite dishes, we'll show you how easy it is for them to be plant-based and still be just as delicious – and we think even tastier!

We'll share our tips for making plant-based cooking simple, with recipes to fit around your lifestyle. This book contains everything you need to get you eating more plants, every day. You'll learn how to prepare unbelievable curries, discover our bangin' burgers, enjoy cheesy pizzas and we'll even let you in on our secret recipe for irresistible finger-licking Wild West Wings. As well as sharing our amazing cakes and desserts. You'll discover loads of new favourite recipes, family feasts, healthy meals and all-time classics.

Everything is set out to help you nail your cooking, so you can find a recipe that works for you whatever you feel like eating, and however much time you have. We'll show you how to make your food taste amazing and look incredible. And, of course, everything is all plants.

Whether you are a veggie, vegan or veg-lover looking for new recipes or to cut down on the amount of meat you eat, we've got you covered. Plants have never tasted this good!

BISH, BASH, BOSH!

We are so happy to have you here in our kitchen! This book is all about you. We've poured our life and soul into this, our second cookbook, for just one purpose: to help you enjoy even more plant-based deliciousness in your life.

Looking back over the past five years, it's incredible to think how much our lives have changed.

Back then, both of us were in a pretty bad place. We were running a tech start-up and things weren't going the way we'd hoped. Long hours and money worries were causing us both incredible amounts of stress. We were friends who worked together in the same team, and we were feeling truly worn down by the grind. Something needed to change.

After deciding to cut out all animal products, we can honestly say we both felt the benefits almost overnight. We felt lighter, had more energy, and felt truly rested for the first time in ages. Plants had saved us!

As lovers of food since an early age and passionate home cooks, we went on a voyage of culinary discovery. And for the next few years we dedicated ourselves to sharing everything we learned about how to make delicious plant-based meals, putting all our tried-and-tested recipes online. And with that, BOSH! was born.

Soon after, we published our first cookbook, and in three years we went from home cooks to bestselling authors with videos that have been watched over a billion times. It's been an incredible time for plant-based food and we're so proud to have played a part.

But our work and passion doesn't stop there! We want *even more* people to see the amazing benefits of eating more plants – both in how you feel and in the positive impact it has on our environment. Plant-based eating not only does you good, but it does the planet good, too.

BISH BASH BOSH! is all about making your life easier. We'll join you in the kitchen every step of the way, showing you how to prep and cook with ease. It's about cooking wonderful meals, with recipes that are really easy to follow and deliver amazing results every time.

x Henry and Ian

This book

In this book, we share all our secret recipes and techniques for cooking incredible meat-free meals with ease. We'll teach you how to nail your prep, ingredients and method in true BISH BASH BOSH! style.

BISH

This book is a celebration of how you can enjoy all your favourite meals using only plants, whether you need a quick meal after a long day or a feast for a party. Whatever the occasion and however much time you have, we have the perfect recipe for you.

Choose from weeknight favourites like Super-Speedy Spaghetti or One-Tray Pasanda. Or try our amazing I-can't-believe-it's-plants dishes like Pulled Jackfruit Sandwich or Faux Gras. Feed a crowd with our incredible curries (see page 16), Seaside Roll or Holy Trinity Louisiana Gumbo, or there are the always-reliable British comfort-food classics, like BOSH! Bangers with Incredible Mash, and our delicious Shepherd's Pie.

BASH

Each recipe is broken down into three parts to make it super-easy to follow: ingredients, a prep list of things to have ready like boiling the kettle or preheating the oven, and a step-by-step method that includes all the prep so you can do it all as you go along.

You'll also find loads of practical tips to make your prep easier, including ideas for making recipes ahead of time and ways you can adapt recipes to work with what you've already got in your cupboards.

We'll teach you the basics of meal planning and meal prep, and show you how to eat the rainbow. You'll also find some brilliant visual indexes to help you navigate the book. Fantastic Feasts will give you inspiration for your favourite dishes – maybe you feel like Italian tonight or you're craving Tex-Mex. And there are dozens of Bonus Recipes like our fail-safe Quick Onion Gravy, Classic Custard and Melty Cashew Cheese, as well as all our favourite dips, sauces and sides. These key recipes provide a reliable and versatile toolkit for anything you want to create in the kitchen.

BOSH!

We want the recipes in the book to help make you feel great simply by eating amazing food, filled with delicious flavours, that's all plants. The recipes are high in fibre and filled with colour, nutrients and joy. You'll discover a new world of flavour and feel lighter, freer and happier in your body and your self.

This book will help you make plant-based meals fit easily into your everyday life, however often you choose to cook them.

Welcome to BISH BASH BOSH!

Your kitchen

Get your cupboards and cook space organised, invest in some essentials and you'll save yourself loads of time in the kitchen while improving your cooking significantly.

FOOD

Keep a well-stocked pantry for meals in minutes. Here are our suggested essentials – top them up whenever you're running low:

balsamic vinegar | basmati rice | coconut milk | dried rice noodles | dried pasta (wholegrain is healthier) | lentils | milled flaxseed | mixed nuts | mixed seeds | olive oil (extra-virgin for dressings and normal for cooking) | peanut butter (shop-bought or keep a stock of your own, see page 266) | plain flour | plant-based milk (fortified with B12) | rapeseed oil | soy sauce | tinned beans | tinned chickpeas | tinned tomatoes | tomato purée

A collection of dried herbs and spices will give you a toolkit of flavour. A great starter selection would be:

black pepper (in a grinder) | chilli flakes | cinnamon | coriander | cumin | curry powder | fennel seeds | oregano | rosemary | thyme | garlic powder | garam masala | ginger | turmeric | hot chilli powder | mixed Italian herbs | onion powder | paprika | sea salt

We put greens with everything, so get in the habit of bringing fresh herbs, fruits and veggies home on a regular basis. We like:

apples | aubergines | avocados | bananas | berries | basil | carrots | chillies | coriander | garlic | ginger | kale | lemons | limes | mushrooms | onions | oranges | parsley | peppers | potatoes | salad greens | spinach | tomatoes

We've always got butter and cheese in the fridge just like we did before, except now they're dairy-free! Our regular fridge items include:

dairy-free butter | dairy-free cheese | dairy-free milk | egg-free mayonnaise | firm tofu | plant-based yoghurt

KIT

The number-one piece of equipment we recommend investing in:

If you're going to be cooking more plant-based meals then we really recommend getting a good-quality, high-powered liquidiser. With one of these you can make creamy sauces, nutrient-filled smoothies, home-made milks and more. And high-powered means high-powered. You want a recent model that's really powerful, with a big jug. If your liquidiser isn't powerful enough to make a completely smooth milk from soaked cashew nuts, get a new one. Trust us, you'll be glad you did.

Here is our list of kit essentials:

baking trays and baking sheets | chopping boards | colander | fine grater or Microplane | foil | food processor (and/or stick blender) | frying pan | heatproof bowl | kitchen timer | knives – at least 3 good quality ones, plus a sharpening steel | measuring jug | measuring spoons | mixing bowls | saucepans – including some good non-stick ones – with tight-fitting lids | sieve | slotted spoon | spatula | storage containers (we prefer glass) | tongs | vegetable peeler | weighing scales | whisk | wooden spoons

We also love to have:

garlic crusher | box grater | griddle pan | oven-to-table serving dishes | rolling pin | tofu press

Organise Your Kitchen, Pantry & Spice Cabinet
We advise you, as over-the-top as it may sound, to label your cupboards and shelves. You can use sticky notes, masking tape or even get a label-maker for twenty quid. Take everything out of your cupboards and off the shelves (food, crockery, pans – everything) and organise it again. Choose a system that works for you and the amount of stuff you own.

Here's how we organise our kitchen:
Breads & Snacks | Flours & Baking | Herbs & Spices | Miscellaneous | Oils & Vinegars | Nuts & Seeds | Pasta, Rice & Grains | Syrups & Sauces | Tins & Jars

Pro Tips: We like all our food stored on open shelves (not in cupboards) so we can see what we have at a glance | Put a blackboard or notepad on a wall (with chalk or a pen) for noting down ingredients you need to restock

Organise Your Cookware, Equipment & Crockery
Having your workspace well organised will help you be speedy with your cooking and make sure you always know where everything is, so you're never reaching to the back of a cupboard for a spoon when you should be stirring your sauce on the stove. Here's roughly how we organise our bits and bobs.

Near where you cook:
Chopping Boards | Cooking Oils | Food processor | Knives & Sharpening Steel | Liquidiser | Pans | Pan Lids (in a separate drawer from pans) | Salt & Pepper | Utensils (hang them for easy access) | Weighing Scales

Not so near where you cook:
Cleaning Stuff & Bin Bags | Foil, Parchment Paper & Freezer Bags | Glasses & Mugs | Measuring Jugs & Mixing Bowls | Plates & Bowls (cereal, wide and serving) | Storage Containers (store with lids on)

Pro Tips: Get your family, friends or flatmates on board with the system (we use a coffee-buying punishment for disobeyers) | Update your system from time to time as your collection grows | Stacking boxes and labels can be really useful for expanding your kitchen in an organised way

Fantastic feasts (and where to find them)

Whatever you're in the mood for, we've got you covered! Fancy some spice? Then check out our Incredible Curries. In need of a health boost, then we have an Eat the Rainbow selection of recipes just for you. Or maybe you want to know how to make plant-based versions of your favourite British classics? Let these collections of recipes inspire you!

ITALIAN FLAVOURS

Here's a selection of our favourite Italian-inspired dishes, with a BOSH! twist.
Super-Speedy Spaghetti (page 32)
Margherita Pizza (page 102)
Classic Lasagne (page 112)

INCREDIBLE CURRIES

This spread of Indian-inspired dishes will spice up any dinner party! Pick your favourites and enjoy a culinary trip across the Indian subcontinent.
One-Tray Pasanda (page 28)
Ian's Delightful Daal & Roti (page 70)
Curry House Jalfrezi (page 74)
Sweet Potato Tikka Masala (page 88)
Henry's Biryani with Coriander Chutney (page 121)
Big Bad Bhajis with Spicy Tomato Chutney (page 169)

SOUTH-EAST ASIAN DELICIOUSNESS

The deep and warming heat of Thailand, Vietnam and Malaysia comes out in this wonderful selection of dishes.
Tom Kha (page 35)
Vietnamese Sticky Tofu (page 36)
Bún Bò Hué (page 68)
Satay Summer Rolls (page 158)
Spicy Thai Salad (page 190)

HIGH PROTEIN

Where do we get our protein? From plants!
These dishes pack a protein punch so you can
munch down knowing that you're giving your
body what it needs after a big gym sesh.

BRITISH CLASSICS

Nothing beats a trip around the UK's classic
dishes. Here's a selection of our favourite meals
and pub classics.

TEX-MEX

If you like your chilli spicy and your avocados
smashed, then we've got you covered!

I CAN'T BELIEVE IT'S PLANTS!

Plants can be super-versatile and we've recreated some of our old favourites in an all plants stylee. Check out this selection and see if you can tell the difference!

Faux Gras (page 39)
Piri Piri Chorizo Bake (page 60)
Seaside Roll (page 115)
Pan-Fried Seitan Steak with Secret Sauce (page 116)
Party Poppers (page 165)
Notting Hill Patties (page 173)

MEDITERRANEAN GOODNESS

Here's a load of deliciousness from in and around the Mediterranean. Packed with earthy spices and robust and fresh flavours.

Turbo Tortilla (page 31)
Greek Gyros (page 58)
Piri Piri Chorizo Bake (page 60)
Ultimate Falafel Wrap (page 77)
Spinach & Ricotta Zucchinioli (page 193)
Romesco Salad (page 202)

AMERICAN CLASSICS

We've travelled all over America and compiled our favourite dishes to share with you. You'll feel like you're in *Grease* while chowing down on dishes from this selection.

Wild West Wings (page 160)
Party Poppers with BOSH! BBQ Sauce (page 165)
BBQ Beans with Mushroom Burnt Ends (page 170)
Texan Potato Salad (page 174)
Crunchy Cali Slaw (page 177)

Bonus recipes

There is a whole host of extra deliciousness hidden in this book in the form of mini-recipes that are contained within the main ones. Turn to this collection of go-to basics and fail-safe classics whenever you're looking for a quick custard or a marinara sauce, a tasty dressing or an awesome dip to BOSH! your daily cooking.

DRESSINGS, SAUCES & GRAVIES

Amazing Pesto
(page 193)

Bang Bang Peanut Dressing
(page 201)

BOSH! Burger Sauce
(page 50)

Chilli Sauce
(page 161)

Herb Oil
(page 127)

Home-Made Chilli Oil
(page 47)

Home-Made Sambal Chilli Sauce
(page 208)

Katsu Sauce
(page 57)

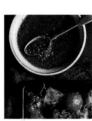
Piri Piri Sauce
(page 60)

Quick Marinara Sauce
(page 102)

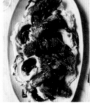
Quick Onion Gravy
(page 97)

Red Wine Gravy
(page 127)

Satay Sauce
(page 158)

Café de Paris Secret Sauce
(page 117)

Speedy Tartare Sauce
(page 84)

20

DIPS, CHUTNEYS & SALSAS

Aioli
(page 178)

Baba Ganoush
(page 197)

Black Bean
Guacamole
(page 47)

Coriander
Chutney
(page 122)

Green Chilli
Guacamole
(page 155)

Home-Made
Turmeric
Hummus
(page 208)

Lemon &
Coriander
Hummus
(page 196)

Mint Raita
(page 107)

Quick Red
Onion Pickle
(page 107)

Quick Salsa
(page 155)

Salsa Verde
(page 115)

Spicy Tomato
Chutney
(page 169)

Tzatziki
(page 58)

BOSH! HACKS

Aubergine Bacon
(page 258)

Balsamic Onions
(page 50)

Carrot Crackling
(page 92)

Cheese: Melty Cashew Cheese
(page 43)

Cheese: Cashew Mozzarella
(page 102)

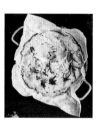
Cheese: Dairy-free Camembert
(page 150)

Eazy Chorizo
(page 61)

Hash Browns
(page 51)

Incredible Mash
(page 96)

Mashy Mashy Peas
(page 84)

Mushroom Burnt Ends
(page 170)

Scrambled Tofu
(page 258)

Sour Cream
(page 155)

SOMETHING SWEET

 **Candied Peanuts** (page 248)

 Caramel Sauce (page 217)

 **Chocolate Buttercream** (page 238)

 Notella Chocolate Hazelnut Spread (page 252)

  **Chocolate Syrup** (page 248)

  **Classic Custard** (page 233)

 **Quick Icing** (page 214)

 **Raspberry Sauce** (page 218)

 **Raspberry Syrup** (page 249)

 **Soft Whipped Cream** (page 249)

 **Vanilla Buttercream** (page 245)

Plan your meals

Meal prepping is becoming increasingly common. It involves planning and cooking a few meals in advance, which saves you loads of time during the week. Some people like to cook enough food for the entire week, but we prefer to keep things as fresh as possible, so we prepare just a couple of days' worth in advance.

We love meal planning and prepping for a number of reasons:

- It gets rid of the annoying 'what's for dinner?' question, reducing the risk of you making unhealthy choices because you're hungry on the way home.

- It helps keep food costs down and reduces waste because all your food is accounted for – and it stops you buying expensive convenience food and ready meals!

- You can take full control of your mealtimes and ensure you're eating healthy, nutritious food.

In this book there are lots of great recipes that can be prepped entirely ahead, such as the salads, curries and pasta dishes, plus plenty more where you can prepare sauces and sides in advance, leaving you only the main meal to make on the day.

Enjoy the freedom from wondering what you are going to eat, make better choices, feel awesome and eat low-cost, high-flavour and nutritious food.

BISH, BASH, BOSH!

Here's how to meal prep for a week, in three easy steps:

1 Plan your week
Think about your week ahead and decide which meals you'd like to make. Make a note of the recipes you've chosen and the days and times you plan to eat them.

Next, carefully read the recipes you want to cook and identify the areas you can prep for. Some recipes can be part-cooked – for example our pasta sauce on page 209 – and you can also make dips, roast veggies, cook grains and make some dishes all the way to the end so that they can just be reheated on the day.

Plan your prep. We prefer to cook just a couple of days' worth of food in advance, but you might like to prep for more days, or even a whole week. Make a note on your meal planner of what you need to prep for each dish – and don't forget to work out how many people you're cooking for each day and adjust the quantities in your recipes accordingly. Then make a shopping list of all your ingredients.

Decide which days you'll be cooking on. We find it easier to get our ingredients online so that we can get everything delivered on the day we prep our meals.

2 Think about how to store your food
Get some airtight containers with tight-fitting lids to store your food in (we prefer glass over plastic) and make sure you have a bag that will fit the containers if you're taking them to work. It's also a good idea to clear some space in your fridge.

3 Cook your food
Now you're ready to actually prep your food! Afterwards, store it in airtight containers in the fridge (make sure to let hot items cool to room temperature before you chill them). Don't forget to label them if you think you might forget what's in each one.

On the day, finish off the dish or reheat it – and don't forget to take your lunch with you to work!

Check out pages 206–9 for a two-day meal plan of delicious recipes.

1

QUICK

Henry's favourite
Piri Piri Chorizo Bake

Ian's favourite
Guacajacks

ONE-TRAY PASANDA

With this wonderful, Anna Jones-inspired recipe you can have a gorgeous, creamy curry on the table in minutes. Or serve it alongside some of our other curries, such as the jalfrezi (see page 74) or our tikka masala (see page 88). If you are cooking a few, get this one in the oven first then lower the heat as you finish off the others. Remove from the oven and stir through the yoghurt.

SERVES 4

1 head cauliflower (about 500g)
500g carrots
2 tbsp vegetable oil
a big pinch of salt
a big pinch of black pepper
1 tsp chilli flakes
1 x 400ml tin full-fat coconut milk
50g ground almonds
2cm piece fresh ginger
2 garlic cloves
1 tsp ground turmeric
1 tsp ground cumin
1 tsp garam masala
½ tsp chilli powder, optional
200g green beans
250g coconut yoghurt
30g flaked almonds
20g fresh coriander

Preheat oven to 180°C | Roasting tin | Grater

First prep and cook the veg | Trim the cauliflower and break it into 3cm florets | If your cauliflower has a lot of good-looking leaves, reserve them to add to the dish near the end | Trim the carrots and cut them into 3cm chunks | Spread the vegetables over a roasting tin and drizzle with the oil | Season with big pinches of salt, pepper and the chilli flakes | Toss to coat the vegetables with the oil and spices | Put the tin in the oven for 15 minutes

Meanwhile, pour the coconut milk into a mixing bowl | Add the ground almonds and stir | Peel the ginger by scraping off the skin with a spoon then finely grate it | Peel and grate the garlic | Add the ginger, garlic, turmeric, cumin, garam masala and chilli powder, if using, to the bowl | Stir everything together until it's really well mixed

After 15 minutes, take the tin out of the oven and pour the coconut paste and green beans over the vegetables | Put the tray back in the oven for 20 minutes, until the cauliflower pieces have started to blacken at the edges | 10 minutes before the end of cooking, add any reserved leaves, if using

Remove the tin from the oven and stir through the coconut yoghurt | Season to taste and add more chilli powder if you like a hotter curry | Sprinkle over the flaked almonds and fresh coriander and serve

TURBO TORTILLA

This is our take on the classic Spanish omelette. It's a great way to use up leftover cooked veggies, so feel free to use whatever you have – just aim for about 400g in total. If you want to up the protein content, replace 100g of the veg with crumbled firm tofu.

SERVES 4

200g waxy new potatoes,
   such as Jersey Royals
100g Tenderstem broccoli
100g asparagus
1 red pepper
100g cherry tomatoes
1 medium red onion
1 garlic clove
1 fresh red chilli
3 tbsp olive oil
175g gram flour
1 tbsp salt
175ml water

Preheat oven to 180°C | Large saucepan | Large baking tray | Large frying pan | Medium frying pan

Wash and thinly slice the potatoes and put them into the saucepan | Fill the pan with cold, salted water and place over a high heat | Bring to the boil and cook for 10 minutes | Drain and set aside

Meanwhile, prepare the rest of your veg | Trim the broccoli and asparagus and cut them into bite-sized pieces | Cut the pepper in half, cut out the stem and seeds and chop into bite-sized chunks | Spread the broccoli, asparagus, pepper and tomatoes evenly over the baking tray | Put the tray in the oven to cook the veggies for 20 minutes

Peel and thinly slice the red onion and garlic | Rip the stem from the chilli, cut it in half lengthways, remove the seeds and finely chop | Put the large frying pan over a medium heat and add 2 tablespoons of the olive oil | Add the onions and sweat, stirring occasionally, for 8–10 minutes, until translucent | Add the garlic and chilli and cook for a further 3–4 minutes | Remove from the heat and set aside

Sift the gram flour and salt into a large bowl | Gradually add the water, whisking constantly until you have a smooth batter (you may not need to use all the water) | Tip all the cooked vegetables into the batter and stir to cover

To cook the tortilla, put the medium frying pan over a medium heat and add 1 tablespoon olive oil | Pour in the batter with all the vegetables and cook for about 20–25 minutes, until the edges are golden and crispy

Gently loosen the edges with a spatula or spoon and remove from the pan, cut it into slices and serve immediately | We love to serve this with a little rocket on the side

SUPER-SPEEDY SPAGHETTI

If you're looking for a really quick and easy spaghetti dish, then look no further! Everything goes into the same pot and the water the pasta cooks in then becomes the sauce. It's saucier than a typical pasta, but it's quick, easy, delicious and we love it!

SERVES 4

1 small red onion
2 garlic cloves
75ml olive oil, plus extra for drizzling
1 tsp salt
400g cherry tomatoes
½ tsp chilli flakes
2 tbsp red wine (or red wine vinegar)
1 litre boiling water
400g spaghetti
a handful of black olives (we like Kalamata)
black pepper
20g fresh basil leaves

Large saucepan with a lid on a medium heat | Kettle boiled | Fine grater or Microplane

First make the tomato sauce | Peel and thinly slice the red onion | Peel and grate the garlic | Pour the olive oil into the saucepan | Add the sliced onion and salt and fry for 5–7 minutes, stirring occasionally, until the onion is soft and translucent | Add the garlic to the pan, stir it in and cook for a further 2 minutes | Add the tomatoes and stir them around for 2 minutes, until the skins start to split | Sprinkle over the chilli flakes and pour in the wine, stirring to coat the tomatoes

Pour the boiling water into the pan | Add the spaghetti, let it soften and then move it around with tongs in the pan until it's well submerged | Put the lid on the pan, turn up the heat and bring to the boil | Take off the lid and cook at a rolling boil for 10–12 minutes, moving the pasta in the water fairly often to ensure it cooks evenly (it's easiest to do this with tongs)

When most of the starchy water has been absorbed by the pasta, taste to make sure it's cooked to your liking | Quickly slice the olives and stir them through the pasta

Divide among bowls, drizzle with olive oil and grind over some black pepper | Garnish with the basil leaves and serve

TOM KHA

A gorgeously spicy coconut soup straight from the streets of Bangkok. Try switching out herbs or flavours to make use of what you've got in the fridge. Swap the onions for shallots, green beans for beansprouts, coriander for Thai basil... Play around and see what works, just keep the base of spices and herbs consistent.

5cm piece fresh ginger
2 lemongrass stalks
4 eschalion (banana) shallots
500g mixed exotic mushrooms
1 red pepper
350g cherry tomatoes
5 bird's-eye chillies
100g green beans
2 x 400ml tins full-fat coconut milk
7 kaffir lime leaves
200ml water
3 tbsp soy sauce
1 tsp coconut sugar
20g fresh coriander
2 spring onions
2 limes

Large saucepan

First prep your veg and aromatics | Peel the ginger by scraping off the skin with a spoon, then thinly slice | Peel the hard outer bark of the lemongrass, roughly chop the tender stalk into three pieces and bash with the heel of a knife | Peel and thinly slice the shallots | If they're big, roughly chop the mushrooms into bite-sized pieces, otherwise leave them as they are

Cut the pepper in half, cut out the stems and seeds and cut the flesh into 2.5cm chunks | Halve the cherry tomatoes | Rip the stems from the chillies or, if you prefer a spicy soup, keep the stems and spilt the chilli down the middle to expose the seeds | Cut the ends off the green beans and slice them in half

Put the saucepan over a medium heat | Pour in half the coconut milk and bring to a gentle simmer | Add the ginger, lemongrass, shallots and lime leaves and stir very gently for 3–4 minutes | Pour in the remaining coconut milk and the water and simmer for 1 minute | Add the mushrooms and chillies and stir gently for 3–4 minutes

Add the green beans to the pan and stir gently for 1 minute | Add the red pepper, cherry tomatoes, soy sauce and coconut sugar and stir gently to mix everything together | Reduce the heat and leave to simmer for 7–8 minutes | Take the pan off the heat

To finish the soup | Rip the leaves from the coriander and chop roughly | Halve and shred the spring onions | Cut the limes in half and squeeze the juice into the soup | Stir two-thirds of the chopped coriander leaves into the soup, reserving the rest, and simmer for 1 minute | Taste and add more soy sauce for saltiness or lime juice for sourness, if needed | Serve, garnished with the reserved coriander leaves and spring onions

VIETNAMESE STICKY TOFU

This recipe is super-quick, packed full of flavour and answers the age-old question, 'what should I do with tofu?' It's a great dinner option if you don't have much time but want something absolutely delicious. Pressing the tofu is really important here as it needs to be the right, firm texture.

SERVES 2

1 x 280g block firm tofu (smoked tofu works well too)

2.5cm piece fresh ginger

1 garlic clove

1 fresh red chilli

4 spring onions

30ml lime juice (about 1½–2 limes)

50g cornflour

vegetable oil, for frying

80g soft brown sugar

4 tbsp soy sauce

160ml coconut water

250g cooked basmati rice, or use 1 x 250g bag microwavable rice, to serve

2 heads pak choi

2 tbsp sesame oil

¼ tsp salt

2 tsp sesame seeds

Tofu press or 2 clean tea towels and a weight such as a heavy book | Fine grater or Microplane | Large frying pan | Line a plate with kitchen paper | Wok | Griddle pan

Press the tofu using a tofu press or place it between two clean tea towels, lay it on a plate and put a weight on top | Leave for at least 30 minutes to drain and firm up before you start cooking

Meanwhile, peel the ginger by scraping off the skin with a spoon and finely grate it | Peel and grate the garlic | Rip the stem from the chilli, cut it in half lengthways and remove the seeds if you prefer, then thinly slice | Finely chop two-thirds of the spring onions | Ribbon the remaining spring onions and keep to one side to garnish | Cut the limes in half

Put the cornflour in a shallow bowl | Cut the drained tofu into 8 slices and roll them evenly in the cornflour to coat

Place the frying pan on a medium-high heat | Pour enough vegetable oil into the pan to cover the base generously | Heat until a wooden spoon dipped into the oil sizzles around the edges | Lay the tofu in the pan and fry for 5–6 minutes, turning halfway | Drain on kitchen paper

Pour 1 tablespoon oil into the wok and place over a high heat | Add the grated ginger and garlic, the chopped spring onions and the sliced chilli | Stir-fry for 90 seconds | Sprinkle over the sugar and stir until a syrup forms | Stir in the soy sauce and coconut water | Bring to a rolling boil and cook for roughly 15 minutes, until the liquid has reduced by two-thirds | Squeeze in the lime juice | Reduce the heat to low

Heat the rice or cook it following the instructions on the packet

To cook the pak choi, put the griddle pan on a high heat | Cut the pak choi into quarters | Put it in a mixing bowl and toss with the sesame oil and salt | Lay the pak choi on the hot griddle pan, cut-side down, and cook until they get black char lines | Transfer to plates

Place the slices of prepared tofu in the wok, one by one, and toss carefully so they're well covered in the sticky sauce

Divide the rice between plates | Top with the sticky tofu | Drizzle over any leftover sauce | Garnish with reserved spring onions and sesame seeds | Serve with the chargrilled pak choi

FAUX GRAS

This amazing recipe was the brainchild of Alexis Gauthier, and was shared with the world through a collaboration we did with him. Spread it on sourdough toast and serve with cornichons for the perfect starter or canapé with drinks – it tastes like proper, posh pâté! If you're eating it straightaway, serve in ramekins, or else store in sterilised jars in the fridge for up to a week.

MAKES 4 SMALL JARS
OR RAMEKINS

2 sprigs fresh rosemary
3 sprigs fresh thyme
7 sage leaves
2 tbsp olive oil
1 eschalion (banana) shallot
a pinch of salt
2 garlic cloves
18 button mushrooms
2 tbsp cognac
150g walnuts
400g cooked lentils (home-made
    or from a packet)
2½ tbsp soy sauce
½ or 1 very small cooked beetroot
    (about 30g)
100g dairy-free butter
a few peppercorns, to garnish
good-quality toasted sourdough bread
    or baguette (or a pack of crackers),
    to serve
cornichons, to serve, optional

4 small sterilised glass jars or ramekins | Frying pan | Food processor | Small saucepan

To sterilise the jars and lids, wash them in hot, soapy water then fill them to the top with boiling water | Drain on a tea towel until completely dry

Remove the leaves from the herbs by running your thumb and forefinger from the top to the base of the stems (the leaves should easily come away) | Reserve a few leaves and sprigs for garnish and finely chop the rest

Pour the oil into the frying pan over a medium heat | Peel and roughly chop the shallot and add it to the pan | Add a pinch of salt and cook for about 7 minutes, stirring occasionally, until translucent

Peel and roughly chop the garlic and add to the pan | Cook for a further 3 minutes | Chop the mushrooms and add them to the pan | Cook, stirring continuously, for 5 minutes, until everything is well softened | Add the finely chopped herbs and the cognac

Transfer the contents of the pan to the food processor | Chop the walnuts and add them to the processor with the cooked lentils, soy sauce and beetroot | Blitz until almost smooth | Transfer the mixture to the prepared jars or ramekins and smooth the tops with the back of a spoon

Place the small saucepan over a low heat | Add the dairy-free butter and melt without heating it too much as it can split | Pour it over the pâté to completely cover | Place a few herb leaves, sprigs and peppercorns on top and leave to cool | Seal the jars (or cover the ramekins with cling film) and refrigerate to chill

Serve with the toasted sourdough bread or crackers and cornichons, if using

GRILLED CHEESE SANDWICHES

We love how quick and satisfying a grilled cheese sandwich is! On the following pages are our three favourite fillings. We've also given you our recipe for dairy-free cheese. Tapioca flour helps the cheese firm up for optimum meltiness — you may need to go to a health food shop to find it, but it'll be worth it (and you can use it in our mozzarella balls on page 102).

AMERICAN CLASSIC SANDWICH

MAKES 4

40g pickled cucumbers or cornichons
8 slices fresh sourdough bread
1 x portion Home-Made Melty Cheese
   (see page 43)
2 tbsp American mustard
2 tbsp tomato ketchup
dairy-free butter, for spreading

Frying pan

Thinly slice the pickles | Generously butter the bread with dairy-free butter | Put the pan on a medium heat

Place one slice of bread in the frying pan, buttered side down | Spread with a quarter of the cheese and lay the pickles on top | Dollop a quarter of the mustard and ketchup on top and spread them out | Place a slice of bread on top, buttered side up | Increase the heat to medium and press the bread down with a spatula until it starts to sizzle, 4–5 minutes

Flip the sandwich over and fry for another 4–5 minutes, until the bread is golden and crispy | Transfer to a chopping board, cut in half and serve immediately | Repeat to make all the sandwiches

ENGLISH PLOUGHMAN'S SANDWICH

MAKES 4

8 slices fresh sourdough bread
dairy-free butter, for spreading
1 x portion Home-Made Melty Cheese
    (see opposite)
4 tbsp pickled chutney

Frying pan on a medium heat

....

Generously butter the bread with dairy-free butter

Place one slice of bread in the frying pan, buttered side down | Spread with a quarter of the cheese | Dollop 1 tablespoon of the chutney over the cheese and spread it around | Place a slice of bread on top, buttered side up | Increase the heat to medium and press the bread down with a spatula until it starts to sizzle, about 4–5 minutes

Flip the sandwich over and fry for another 4–5 minutes, until the bread is golden and crispy | Transfer to a chopping board, cut in half and serve immediately | Repeat to make all the sandwiches

INDIAN-STYLE CHUTNEY SANDWICH

MAKES 4

1 spring onion
8 slices fresh sourdough bread
dairy-free butter, for spreading
1 x portion Home-Made Melty Cheese
    (see opposite)
4 tbsp brinjal (aubergine) pickle

Frying pan

....

Thinly slice the spring onion | Generously butter the bread with dairy-free butter | Put the pan over a medium heat

Place a slice of bread in the frying pan, buttered side down | Spread with a quarter of the cheese | Dollop 1 tablespoon of the brinjal pickle over the cheese | Sprinkle over a quarter of the spring onion | Place a slice of bread on top, buttered side up | Increase the heat to medium and press the bread down with a spatula until it starts to sizzle, about 4–5 minutes

Flip the sandwich over and fry for another 4–5 minutes, until the bread is golden and crispy | Transfer to a chopping board, cut in half and serve immediately | Repeat to make all the sandwiches

HOME-MADE MELTY CHEESE

This cheese has a delicious gooey consistency, particularly when melted, making it perfect for grilled cheese sandwiches. The recipe makes more than you need for the sandwiches so keep the leftovers in the fridge for a couple of days.

MAKES 250–300g

60g cashews
1 carrot (about 75g)
500ml water
1 small garlic clove
150ml aquafaba (the drained water from
    1–2 x 400g tins chickpeas)
2 tbsp tapioca flour
1 tbsp coconut oil
½ tsp salt, plus more to taste
2 tbsp nutritional yeast
¼ lemon
black pepper, to taste

Small saucepan | Liquidiser

First cook the cashews and carrot | Peel and finely chop the carrot | Put the cashews in the saucepan with the carrot and cover them with the water | Put the pan over a high heat, bring to the boil and cook for 20 minutes | Take off the heat, save 300ml of the cooking liquid then drain the cashews and carrot | Peel the garlic

Now combine all the ingredients together | Put the cashews, carrot, garlic, aquafaba, tapioca flour, coconut oil, salt, nutritional yeast and the reserved cooking liquid into the liquidiser | Squeeze in the lemon juice, catching any pips in your other hand | Blend until you have a smooth cream

Pour the cream back into the saucepan, taste and season with salt and pepper | Put the pan over a medium heat and cook, stirring constantly, for 5–6 minutes, until the cheese has a thick, homogenous texture | Pour into a bowl, cover, leave to cool then refrigerate until needed

SINGAPORE FRIED VERMICELLI

Quick, satisfying and spicy, this is perhaps our favourite ever noodle dish. It is the perfect accompaniment to an Asian feast. Try it with our Vietnamese Sticky Tofu (see page 36) or Speedy Hoisin Mushrooms (see page 64). Feel free to freestyle on the veg – this is a great fridge-raid recipe.

SERVES 4–6

4 garlic cloves
150g fresh mushrooms
4 spring onions
3 fresh red chillies
100g Tenderstem broccoli
1 head pak choi (about 100g)
1 large carrot
1 red pepper
250g dried rice vermicelli
4 tbsp vegetable oil
4½ tbsp soy sauce
2 tsp curry powder
1 tbsp sugar
2 tbsp water
a pinch of salt
a pinch of black pepper
1 lime

Kettle boiled | Fine grater or Microplane | Peeler | Wok

Get all the veggies ready to stir-fry | Peel and grate the garlic | Thinly slice the mushrooms and spring onions | Rip the stems from two of the chillies, cut them in half lengthways, removing the seeds if you prefer less heat, then finely chop | Chop the broccoli into 2cm pieces | Trim the pak choi and separate the leaves | Peel the carrot and then use the peeler to slice long, thin ribbons | Cut the pepper in half and cut out the stem and seeds, then slice into thin strips

Prepare the vermicelli following the instructions on the packet | Keep checking them as you want the noodles to still be a little firm when you add them to the wok, as they will carry on cooking

Put the wok on a high heat and add the oil | Once the pan is really hot, add the garlic, chopped chillies and mushrooms | Stir-fry for 30 seconds, then add the rest of the veg | Stir in the soy sauce, curry powder and sugar and stir-fry for a further 2 minutes | Drain the noodles and stir them through the veggies | Add the water

Season with the salt and pepper | Cut the lime in half and squeeze in the juice, to taste | Rip the stem from the remaining chilli, thinly slice and scatter over the top

GUACAJACKS

Ian came up with the name for this and now the Guacajack shall live on forever as an incredibly easy, delicious meal that we make all the time. We've given traditional guac a special BOSH! treatment with added black beans for extra bite and a bonus protein boost, with chopped cherry tomatoes and shallots for freshness.

SERVES 2

2 large sweet potatoes
2 tbsp chilli oil (shop-bought or make our Home-Made Chilli Oil, see below)
salt

FOR THE BLACK BEAN GUACAMOLE
2 small ripe avocados
1 small eschalion (banana) shallot
½ garlic clove
1 small fresh red chilli
6 cherry tomatoes
1 lime
15g fresh coriander
½ x 400g tin black beans
1 tbsp olive oil, optional

Preheat oven to 180°C | **Line a baking tray with parchment paper** | **Fine grater or Microplane** | **Saucepan**

Put the sweet potatoes on the baking tray and pierce them a few times with a fork | Rub the potatoes with the chilli oil and a generous pinch of salt | Put the tray in the oven and bake for 50–55 minutes, until the skin has begun to crisp up and the flesh is tender

When the potatoes are nearly cooked, make your guac | Halve and carefully stone the avocados by tapping the stone firmly with the heel of a knife so that it lodges in the stone, then twist and remove | Spoon the flesh into a mixing bowl and mash with a fork | Peel and finely chop the shallot | Peel and grate the garlic | Rip the stem from the chilli, cut it in half lengthways and remove the seeds, then finely chop | Finely chop the cherry tomatoes | Add the shallots, garlic, chilli and tomatoes to the bowl | Halve the lime and squeeze in the juice | Fold everything together to combine | Taste and season with salt | Pick the leaves from the coriander and discard the stems | Set aside a third of the leaves for garnish then finely chop the rest and add to the bowl | Drain and rinse the black beans and stir them into the guacamole | If the consistency is a little stiff, add a little olive oil to soften it

Take the tray out of the oven and leave the potatoes to cool for 5 minutes | Carefully slice open the sweet potatoes and gently fluff the flesh with a fork | Spoon half the guacamole into each potato | Garnish with the reserved coriander leaves and serve immediately

HOME-MADE CHILLI OIL

MAKES 250ml

250ml + 2 tbsp light olive oil
4 dried ancho chillies
3 tsp chilli flakes

Sterilised bottle or jar (see page 39)

Pour the 2 tablespoons oil into the pan and heat | Add the chillies and flakes and stir for 1 minute | Pour in the rest of the oil, turn the heat right down and warm through for about 5 minutes, being careful not to let the oil bubble | Take off the heat and cool to room temperature | Pour into the bottle or jar and screw on the lid | Use within 1 month

QUICK QUESADILLAS

There's nothing like a little Mexican food to get the day moving along just right! The quesadilla is like the Mexican version of a toasted sandwich, so it's only right we gave it our full attention. Use wholegrain or corn-based tortillas if you are cutting down on processed wheat flour. These are also great served with a simple tomato salad.

1 red onion
1 garlic clove
2 large roasted red peppers from a jar
100g dairy-free cheese
1 large avocado
30g fresh coriander
1 lime
1 x 400g tin black beans (or kidney beans)
2 tbsp + 1 tsp olive oil
1 x 400g tin chopped tomatoes
1 tsp cayenne pepper, plus a little more
100g tinned sweetcorn
4 large flour tortillas
salt and black pepper

Fine grater or Microplane | 2 large frying pans

First get all your ingredients ready | Peel and thinly slice the red onion | Peel and grate the garlic | Cut the roasted red peppers into strips | Grate the dairy-free cheese | Halve and carefully stone the avocado by tapping the stone firmly with the heel of a knife so that it lodges in the stone, then twist and remove | Scoop out the flesh and cut into small chunks | Pick the leaves from the coriander and chop finely | Cut the lime half | Drain and rinse the beans

Place a frying pan on a medium heat | Add 2 tablespoons olive oil | Add the onion to the hot pan with a pinch of salt and sweat for 7–8 minutes, until softened | Add the garlic and stir for 1–2 minutes | Add the roasted red pepper strips, black beans, tomatoes and 1 teaspoon cayenne pepper and cook for 5 minutes | Remove from the heat and stir in the sweetcorn | Taste and season with salt and pepper | Add more cayenne if you want more heat | Squeeze over the lime juice

Put the second pan on a medium heat | Add 1 teaspoon oil | Lay a tortilla in the pan and sprinkle over a generous handful of grated cheese | Spoon a quarter of the filling on to the tortilla and spread it over one half | Sprinkle avocado and coriander on top of the filling

Once the cheese has melted, check the underside of the tortilla – if golden cooking spots are appearing, the quesadilla is ready | Use a spatula to fold it in half, sandwiching the filling | Remove from the pan, slice into wedges and serve immediately | Repeat to make all the quesadillas

BANGIN' BURGERS

Here are a couple of bangin' quick burgers, inspired by our travels to Ibiza, for Addison's stag, and L.A. The brilliant balsamic onions and classic burger sauce are great with everything BBQ and the hash browns in the L.A. burger add an amazing extra layer of flavour and texture. Customise your burger, just be sure to migrate beyond ketchup and lettuce!

IBIZA SUNSET BURGER

SERVES 2

2 plant-based burger patties, or The Big BOSH! Burgers from our first book, *BOSH!*, page 119
2 slices dairy-free cheese
2 pickled gherkins
1 baby gem lettuce
2 good-quality burger buns

FOR THE BALSAMIC ONIONS
1 large red onion
1 tbsp olive oil
2 tsp soft brown sugar
2 tsp balsamic vinegar

FOR THE BOSH! BURGER SAUCE
50g egg-free mayonnaise
1 tbsp gherkin brine (from the jar)
½ tsp maple syrup
¼ tsp vinegar
¼ tsp white pepper
½ tsp Dijon mustard
¼ tsp onion powder
¼ tsp garlic powder
¼ tsp smoked paprika

Preheat oven to 180°C | Line a baking tray | Frying pan on a low heat | Roasting tin

First make the Balsamic Onions | Peel and thinly slice the red onion | Add the olive oil to the frying pan on a low heat | Add the onion and fry for 12–15 minutes, stirring occasionally, until lightly browned | Add the sugar and balsamic vinegar and stir for 3–4 minutes, until the sugar has dissolved and the onions have darkened | Take the pan off the heat

Put the burger patties on the lined baking tray | Put the tray in the oven and cook following the instructions on the packet | 5 minutes before they're ready, lay a slice of dairy-free cheese on top of each patty and place an upturned roasting tin over the patties to stop the cheese drying out | Bake for the remaining 5 minutes

Meanwhile, make the BOSH! Burger Sauce by combining all the ingredients in a small bowl and mixing together with a fork

Slice the gherkins | Shred the lettuce

Assemble your burgers! Slice the burger buns in half and spread the bottoms with the BOSH! Burger Sauce | Take the burgers and cheese out of the oven and place one patty on each burger bun | Top the cheese with the shredded lettuce and sliced gherkins and then pile on the balsamic onions | Close the lids of the burgers and serve

L.A. GUACBURGER

SERVES 2

2 plant-based burger patties, or
    The Big BOSH! Burgers from our
    first book, *BOSH!*, page 119
4 slices dairy-free cheese
2 good-quality burger buns
2 tbsp egg-free mayonnaise
4 baby gem lettuce leaves
1 large tomato

FOR THE GUACAMOLE
1 lime
1 small garlic clove
¼ tsp salt
1 large ripe avocado
1 small fresh red chilli
2 spring onions
4 cherry tomatoes
10g fresh coriander

FOR THE HASH BROWNS
1 large potato
2 tbsp plain flour
¾ tsp salt
¼ tsp black pepper
olive oil, for shallow frying

Preheat oven to 180°C | **Fine grater or Microplane** | **Clean tea towel** | **Frying pan** | **Line a plate with kitchen paper** | **Line a baking tray** | **Roasting tin**

First make the guacamole | Halve the lime and squeeze the juice into a bowl | Peel and grate the garlic into the bowl | Add the salt | Halve and carefully stone the avocado by tapping the stone firmly with the heel of a knife so that it lodges in the stone, then twist and remove | Scoop the flesh into the bowl | Use the back of a fork to mash everything together

Rip the stem from the chilli, cut it in half lengthways, remove the seeds and finely chop | Trim and finely chop the spring onions and cherry tomatoes and add them to the bowl | Pick the leaves from the coriander, roughly chop and add them to the bowl | Stir all the ingredients together with a fork so they're well mixed | Taste and add a little more seasoning if necessary | Cover and refrigerate

Peel the potato for the Hash Browns and grate it into a sieve | Wash under cold water until the water runs clear | Tip into the clean tea towel and twist the towel over the sink to squeeze out all the excess moisture | Put the grated potato into a mixing bowl | Sprinkle over the flour, salt and pepper and mix everything together | Roll the grated potato into 2 balls and squash them into 1cm-thick patties

Put the frying pan over a medium heat | Pour in the olive oil until it's 1cm deep | Warm until a wooden spoon dipped into the oil sizzles around the edges | Carefully place the hash browns in the oil and cook for 3–4 minutes on each side, until golden brown and crispy | Transfer to the plate lined with kitchen paper to drain

Put the burger patties on the lined baking tray | Put the tray in the oven and cook following the instructions on the packet | 5 minutes before they're ready, lay a slice of dairy-free cheese and a hash brown on top of each patty and place an upturned roasting tin over the patties to stop the cheese drying out | Bake for the remaining 5 minutes

To assemble the burgers, slice the buns in half and spread the bottoms with the egg-free mayo | Cover with 2 lettuce leaves for each bun | Cut the tomato into thick slices and lay them over the lettuce | Take the burgers, cheese and hash browns out of the oven and place one patty on each burger | Dollop the guacamole over the tops | Close the lids of the burgers and serve

Pictured on pages 52–53

L.A. GUACBURGER

IBIZA SUNSET
BURGER

L.A. GUACBURGER

BROCCAULIFLOWER CHEESE

An easy, punchy, gorgeously warming dish that is perfect for a winter evening. As it's packed with veggies and low on processed carbs it's also not too heavy. Feel free to roast any veggies you like to add to this bake. The roux used in this dish is really reliable and would work well in any creamy pasta bake.

SERVES 4

1 head cauliflower (about 600g)
1 head broccoli (about 350g)
1½ tbsp olive oil
100g fresh spinach leaves
50g panko breadcrumbs
fresh chives, to garnish, optional
200g salad, to serve
salt and black pepper

FOR THE CHEESY SAUCE
50g dairy-free butter
50g plain flour
700ml unsweetened plant-based milk
200g dairy-free cheese
25g nutritional yeast
30g pickled jalapeños
1½ tsp garlic powder
¾ tsp smoked paprika
2½ tsp English mustard

Preheat oven to 180°C | Line a baking tray | Large saucepan on a medium heat | Whisk | Grater | 20 x 30cm lasagne dish

....

Trim the cauliflower and broccoli and cut into small florets | Cut the stems into similar-sized pieces | Spread over the lined baking tray | Sprinkle over a little salt, pepper and 1 tablespoon olive oil | Put the tray in the oven and bake for 20–25 minutes

Meanwhile, make the cheesy sauce | Put the dairy-free butter into the medium hot saucepan and stir with a wooden spoon until it melts, then gradually add the flour to the pan, stirring vigorously until you have a doughy paste | Gradually pour in 500ml of the milk, whisking all the time until you have a thick, creamy sauce

Grate the dairy-free cheese | Add the cheese, nutritional yeast, jalapeños, garlic powder, paprika and mustard to the pan, stirring constantly, until the cheese has melted and combined with the sauce | Add the rest of the milk and keep stirring until the sauce has a thick, creamy consistency | Taste, season to perfection with salt and pepper and turn the heat right down

Take the tray out of the oven and turn on the grill to hot | Add the cauliflower and broccoli to the pan of cheese sauce | Add the spinach and fold so that everything is well covered in sauce | Pour into the lasagne dish and smooth out with the back of a wooden spoon

Pour the panko breadcrumbs into a dish and drizzle over the remaining ½ tablespoon olive oil | Toss to coat | Sprinkle the breadcrumbs over the top of the cheesy vegetables

Put the lasagne dish under the grill until golden, 1–5 minutes depending on your grill, so watch it closely | Remove the dish from the oven | Spoon into bowls | Snip over the chives to garnish, if using, and serve with the salad on the side

AUBERGINE KATSU

We've been refining this dish for some time now to achieve the perfect balance of a beautifully light but comfortingly warm katsu sauce. Katsu is amazing with the mighty aubergine. You can also make double the sauce and freeze half, it will keep for a month (defrost it overnight in the fridge before reheating).

SERVES 4

175g plain flour
½ tbsp salt
250ml unsweetened plant-based milk
150g panko breadcrumbs
2 aubergines (about 300g each)
4 spring onions
white sesame seeds, for sprinkling
500g cooked basmati rice, or use
   2 x 250g bags microwavable
   basmati rice, to serve
vegetable oil, for frying

FOR THE KATSU SAUCE
1 large onion
1 small carrot
5cm piece fresh ginger
2 garlic cloves
2 tbsp sesame oil
1 tbsp olive oil
1½ tsp soy sauce
1 tbsp curry powder
350ml vegetable stock
1 lemon
2 tsp garam masala
1 tsp sugar
1 tbsp cornflour
2 tbsp water

Fine grater or Microplane | 2 large frying pans | Liquidiser | Whisk | Line a large plate with kitchen paper

First make the sauce | Peel and dice the onion | Peel and grate the carrot | Peel the ginger by scraping off the skin with a spoon, then finely grate | Peel and grate the garlic

Put one frying pan over a medium heat and warm the sesame oil | Add the onion and fry for 3–4 minutes, stirring | Add the carrot and olive oil and stir for 5–6 minutes | Add the garlic and ginger and stir for 2 minutes | Add the soy sauce and curry powder and stir for 2 minutes, then transfer to the liquidiser along with the vegetable stock | Blend | Pour back into the pan and return to a medium heat

Cut the lemon in half and squeeze the juice of half into the same pan, catching any pips with your other hand | Sprinkle over the garam masala and sugar and stir | Reduce the heat to low | Taste and add more salt and lemon if required | Put the cornflour and water into a small dish and mix together with a fork | Pour into the pan and stir to thicken

Now make the batter | Put the flour, salt and milk into a mixing bowl and whisk to a smooth batter | Tip the breadcrumbs into a separate bowl

Trim the aubergines and cut into 1cm-thick slices | Tip them into the batter and toss to coat | Pick out one slice and roll it around in the breadcrumbs, covering it completely | Repeat to coat all the slices

Fry the aubergine | Pour the vegetable oil into the second pan until it's 2cm deep | Put the pan over a medium heat and heat until a wooden spoon dipped into the oil starts to bubble around the edges | Carefully add the aubergine slices and fry in batches for 3–4 minutes on each side, until crispy and deep golden | Transfer to the kitchen paper for a minute to soak up any excess oil

Meanwhile, heat the rice, if necessary, or cook following the instructions on the packet, then divide among plates | Arrange the crispy aubergine on top and drizzle over the katsu sauce | Thinly slice the spring onions and sprinkle them over with the sesame seeds before serving

GREEK GYROS

Tzatziki is a wonderful dip for things like nachos and crudités or simply spread over bread, so make an extra batch of it to use in another meal. You can make these mushrooms a day ahead and reheat them. If you don't fancy bread, this would make a really great salad box.

SERVES 4

2 red onions
2 garlic cloves
400g shiitake mushrooms
3 tbsp olive oil
2 tbsp red wine vinegar
2 tsp dried oregano
1 tsp dried thyme
1 tsp dried rosemary
½ tsp smoked paprika
½ tsp sugar
1 tsp salt
1 large tomato
½ head baby gem lettuce
4 Greek pitta breads (roughly 20cm in diameter)

FOR THE TZATZIKI
½ cucumber
1½ tbsp salt
1 lemon
1 small garlic clove
4 fresh mint leaves
10g fresh dill
200g thick coconut yoghurt
a drizzle of olive oil
salt and black pepper

Fine grater or Microplane | 2 frying pans | Clean tea towel | Cut out 4 23 x 23cm squares of parchment paper

First make the tzatziki | Peel the cucumber and grate it into a bowl | Sprinkle over the salt and stir to coat | Set aside for 15 minutes

Peel and thinly slice the onions for your gyros | Peel and grate the garlic | Cut the mushrooms into 1cm-thick strips

Put a frying pan over a medium heat and pour in 2 tablespoons olive oil | Add half the sliced onion and fry for 3–4 minutes | Add the garlic and stir for 2 minutes | Add the remaining olive oil | Tip in the mushrooms and stir them into the onions for 3–4 minutes | Add the red wine vinegar, oregano, thyme, rosemary, paprika, sugar and salt | Fold everything together and cook for 7–8 minutes | Reduce the heat to low and keep warm, stirring occasionally

To finish the tzatziki, tip the cucumber into the middle of a clean tea towel, gather up the edges and squeeze out the excess water | Put the strained cucumber back into the bowl | Cut the lemon in half and squeeze over the juice of one half, catching any pips in your other hand | Peel the garlic and finely grate it into the bowl | Finely chop the mint leaves and dill and add them to the bowl | Pour over the coconut yoghurt and mix everything together with a spoon | Taste and season with more lemon juice, if necessary, salt, pepper and a drizzle of olive oil

Thinly slice the tomato | Shred the lettuce

Warm the pitta breads | Put the second frying pan over a medium heat | Gently warm the pitta breads in the pan for a minute on each side

Lay the squares of parchment paper on a clean surface and put a pitta on each one | Spread with a generous helping of tzatziki | Top with the lettuce, tomato slices, an equal serving of the mushroom mixture and the rest of the sliced onion | Wrap your gyros up in the parchment paper and serve immediately

PIRI PIRI CHORIZO BAKE

This is a quick and easy to knock up, eat-the-rainbow revelation. Coloured heritage tomatoes are a great addition if you can get hold of them. The piri piri sauce is wonderful, so consider making double and keeping half for another recipe. Serve with brown rice for an even healthier meal.

SERVES 4

2 medium sweet potatoes
olive oil
1 lemon
1 red pepper
1 green pepper
1 yellow pepper
3 garlic cloves
300g Eazy Chorizo (see opposite) or
   shop-bought veggie chorizo sausages
20 cherry tomatoes
20g fresh coriander
500g cooked basmati rice, or use
   2 x 250g bags microwavable
   basmati rice, to serve
salt and black pepper

FOR THE PIRI PIRI SAUCE
1 red onion
4 garlic cloves
1 red pepper
2 fresh red chillies (scotch bonnet,
   red or bird's-eye)
2 tbsp smoked paprika
1 tsp dried oregano
2 tbsp red wine vinegar
a large bunch of fresh basil
1 lemon

Preheat oven to 180°C | Large microwaveable bowl, optional | Roasting tin | Liquidiser | Fine grater or Microplane

First cook the sweet potatoes | Peel the sweet potatoes and cut them into 2cm cubes | Put them in a large microwaveable bowl, sprinkle over a pinch of salt and pepper and drizzle with olive oil | Cut the lemon in half and squeeze over the juice, catching any pips in your other hand | Toss to coat | Cover the bowl with a plate and microwave on high for 6 minutes, until soft | Alternatively, cook in the oven at 180°C for 30–35 minutes, until soft

Cut the peppers in half, cut out the stems and seeds and cut the flesh into 2cm cubes, then put them in the roasting tin | Use the back of a knife to lightly crush the 3 garlic cloves and add them to the tin | Drizzle over a little olive oil and sprinkle with salt and pepper | Add the sweet potatoes to the peppers and put the tin in the oven for 10–15 minutes, until the peppers have small black patches on the skins

Meanwhile, make the Eazy Chorizo sausages following the recipe opposite (or cut up shop-bought sausages into bite-sized pieces and cook following the instructions on the packet)

To make the piri piri sauce, peel and roughly chop the onion and garlic | Cut the pepper in half and cut out the stem and seeds | Rip the stems from the chillies, cut them in half lengthways and remove the seeds if you prefer a milder sauce | Put the onion, garlic, pepper and chillies in the liquidiser with the paprika, oregano, red wine vinegar and basil | Grate in the zest of the lemon, then cut it in half and squeeze in the juice, catching any pips | Add a drop of water and blend to a smooth paste | Taste and adjust the seasoning, if necessary

Remove the roasting tin from the oven | Transfer the sausages and piri piri sauce to the tin and mix everything together | Add the cherry tomatoes and put the tin back in the oven for 15 minutes, until the potatoes and peppers are cooked and the sauce is piping hot

Heat the rice or cook it following the instructions on the packet

Pluck the leaves from the coriander and dispose of the stems | Coarsely chop the leaves and sprinkle them over the vegetables | Serve with rice

Pictured on pages 62–63

EAZY CHORIZO

Once we'd developed this quick DIY chorizo recipe we never looked back. Hitting a standard shop-bought veggie sausage with fennel, paprika, red wine and maple syrup gives an instant chorizo vibe.

MAKES 300g

300g plant-based sausages
2 tbsp olive oil
1½ tsp smoked paprika
½ tsp cayenne pepper
¼ tsp ground fennel
a pinch of salt
a pinch of black pepper
2 garlic cloves
4 tbsp red wine
½ tbsp maple syrup

Medium frying pan on a medium-high heat | Fine grater or Microplane

Slice the sausages into 2cm-thick rounds | Put them in the hot pan and pour over the olive oil | Fry for 5 minutes, turning them now and again, until golden | Sprinkle over the paprika, cayenne pepper, fennel, salt and pepper | Peel and finely grate the garlic into the pan and fry for another 2 minutes

Carefully add the red wine and maple syrup to the pan and cook until the wine has reduced and you have a sticky glaze, stirring occasionally | Toss to ensure the sausage is covered | Take off the heat once all the liquid in the pan has evaporated, and serve

SPEEDY HOISIN MUSHROOMS

Did you know 'hoisin' means 'seafood'? And yet it neither contains seafood nor is traditionally served with seafood. Either way, we love it. From our first experiences of crispy pancakes to wonderful hoisin stir-fries, it remains a firm favourite. Try subbing the pak choi for gem lettuce or pair with brown rice and greens for a healthy lunchbox.

SERVES 4

2 garlic cloves
4cm piece fresh ginger
15g fresh coriander
6 spring onions
500g mixed mushrooms
2 heads pak choi
3 tbsp sesame oil
1 tbsp rapeseed oil
1½ tbsp soy sauce
2½ tbsp hoisin sauce
1 tbsp sriracha
4 tsp white sesame seeds
500g cooked basmati rice,
    or use 2 x 250g microwavable
    basmati rice, to serve

Fine grater or Microplane | Wok | Griddle pan

Peel and grate the garlic into a small bowl | Peel the ginger by scraping off the skin with a spoon, then grate into the bowl

Separate the coriander leaves and stems and thinly slice both | Thinly slice the spring onions | Roughly chop the mushrooms into bite-sized pieces

Cut the pak choi lengthways into quarters, put them in a mixing bowl and toss with 2 tablespoons of the sesame oil

Add the remaining 1 tablespoon of sesame oil and the rapeseed oil to the wok and set over a medium heat | When the oil is hot, add three-quarters of the spring onions, the garlic, ginger and chopped coriander stems | Fry for 2 minutes, stirring constantly | Add the mushrooms and continue to stir for 6–7 minutes | Add the soy, hoisin and sriracha sauces and stir for 1 minute, making sure the mushrooms are well coated | Turn the heat right down while you cook your pak choi

Put the griddle pan on the maximum heat | While the pan is heating up, heat the rice, if necessary, or cook following the instructions on the packet

Lay the pak choi on the griddle and cook until char lines appear, trying not to move them around too much | Turn and cook the other sides

Divide the rice among bowls | Nestle the pak choi alongside | Spoon over the hoisin mushrooms | Sprinkle over the remaining spring onions, coriander leaves and sesame seeds and serve

2

Henry's favourite
Curry House Jalfrezi

Ian's favourite
Shepherd's Pie

BÚN BÒ HUÉ

After travelling around South-east Asia this dish became Henry's firm favourite. It's a fiery broth, but there's something about this soup that allows you to handle much more heat than you would expect! Double up the broth if you have a pan big enough and freeze half, ready to defrost when you are ready for a really quick soup.

SERVES 4

4 fresh bird's-eye or finger chillies
1 lime
2 spring onions
200g mixed mushrooms
200g glass noodles
200g beansprouts
4 heads mini pak choy
30g fresh mint
30g fresh coriander
30g Thai basil

FOR THE BROTH
1 onion
1 lemongrass stalk
7.5cm piece fresh ginger
6 garlic cloves
100g pineapple (fresh or tinned)
1 green apple
1 fresh red chilli (we prefer bird's-eye
    or finger chillies, but be warned that
    they're hot!)
5g dried shiitake mushrooms (or use
    dried porcini)
5 kaffir lime leaves
2 star anise
3 tbsp coconut sugar
1 litre cold water
150ml soy sauce
salt and black pepper

FOR THE CHILLI SAUCE
1 long lemongrass stalk
2 eschalion (banana) shallots
2 garlic cloves
35ml rapeseed oil
½ tbsp chilli flakes
½ tbsp chilli powder
1 tbsp soy sauce
2 tbsp water
1 tsp maple syrup

1 large stock pot | Fine grater or Microplane | Small frying pan

First make the broth | Peel and halve the onion | Chop the lemongrass in half and lightly bash it with the base of a knife to release the oils | Peel the ginger by scraping off the skin with a spoon and slice | Peel and slice the garlic | Chop the pineapple into chunks | Peel and core the apple and chop roughly | Slice the chilli lengthways | Put all the broth ingredients into the stock pot over a medium-high heat | Bring to the boil and simmer briskly until half the liquid has evaporated | Use a slotted spoon or sieve to remove all the solid ingredients and discard | Taste, season with salt and pepper and set aside

To make the chilli sauce, peel and discard the hard outer bark of the lemongrass and thinly slice | Peel and mince the shallots | Peel and finely grate the garlic | Pour the rapeseed oil into the frying pan and place it on a medium-low heat | Add the sliced lemongrass to the pan and stir for 2 minutes | Add the shallots and stir for 2 minutes | Add the garlic and stir for 1 minute | Add the chilli flakes and chilli powder and stir for 1 minute | Add the soy sauce, water and maple syrup and fry for 1 minute | Reduce the heat to a gentle simmer and cook for 3–5 minutes to reduce and thicken | Take off the heat

Prepare the garnishes | Thinly slice the chillies | Quarter the lime | Trim and thinly slice the spring onions | Chop the mushrooms into bite-sized pieces

Put the broth back on the heat and bring to the boil, then reduce to a gentle simmer | Add the mushrooms and cook for 4 minutes | Add the noodles and cook in the broth following the instructions on the packet

Divide the mushrooms and noodles among bowls | Add 2 teaspoons of the chilli sauce to each bowl | Ladle over the broth | Add the beansprouts, pak choy, mint, coriander and Thai basil leaves | Garnish with the chopped chillies, spring onions and lime wedges | Serve immediately

IAN'S DELIGHTFUL DAAL & ROTI

This is a certified hug-in-a-bowl, and is perhaps one of the finest flavour symphonies we've created. The spice blend is simple but perfectly balanced, and complements the rest of the ingredients. The daal tastes just as good the day after, reheated to piping hot, and the rotis will keep on a plate wrapped in cling film for a couple of days, so definitely make more than you need!

SERVES 4

1 large onion
30g fresh coriander
3 garlic cloves
2.5cm piece fresh ginger
2½ tbsp olive oil
½ tsp salt
1 tsp chilli flakes
½ tbsp ground cumin
1 tsp ground turmeric
4 tsp garam masala
1 tsp caster sugar
1 tsp ground coriander
1 tsp ground fenugreek
200g dried red lentils
1 x 400g tin chopped tomatoes
500ml vegetable stock
1 x 400ml tin full-fat coconut milk
75ml boiling water, optional

FOR THE ROTI
200g self-raising flour, plus extra
    for dusting
½ tsp salt
1 tbsp vegetable oil
100ml water
vegetable oil, for frying

Brush some cling film with oil | Fine grater or Microplane | Large saucepan | Frying pan | Rolling pin or clean, dry wine bottle

......

Start by making the roti | Pour the flour, salt and oil into a large mixing bowl | Make a small well in the centre and pour in the water | Use your hands to mix the ingredients together and knead until it comes together in a smooth ball of dough | Cover the bowl with the oiled cling film and set it aside to rest for 20 minutes

Meanwhile, peel and finely chop the onion | Rip the leaves from the coriander | Finely chop the stems and roughly chop the leaves | Peel and finely grate the garlic | Peel the ginger by scraping off the skin with a spoon and grate finely

Pour the olive oil into the saucepan and warm it over a medium heat | Add the chopped onion and salt and stir for 5–7 minutes, until softened | Add the garlic, ginger, chilli flakes and coriander stems to the pan and stir for 2–3 minutes | Add the cumin, turmeric, garam masala, caster sugar, ground coriander and fenugreek and stir together for 30 seconds

Rinse the lentils and tip them into the pan | Stir for 1 minute | Pour in the chopped tomatoes, fold them into the lentils and bring the thick sauce to a gentle simmer | Pour in the vegetable stock and coconut milk and stir all the ingredients together until well mixed | Bring back to a very gentle simmer, put the lid on the pan and leave it to bubble away for 35–40 minutes until thickened, stirring every now and then to make sure the daal doesn't catch on the bottom of the pan

While the daal is cooking, return to the roti | Take the dough out of the bowl and divide it into 8 equal pieces | Place the pieces of dough on a chopping board and cover with the oiled cling film | Dust a clean surface with flour, take a piece of dough and roll it out into a neat, flat circle, as thin as you can get it | Repeat with the remaining pieces

Put the frying pan over a high heat until very hot | Pour 1 teaspoon oil into the pan and swish it around to coat the base | Place a roti in the pan and cook until it starts to bubble, then flip it over and fry the other side for another minute | Transfer to a plate and repeat to cook all the roti

Once your daal is cooked, take the lid off the pan, taste it and season as necessary | If the lentils have too much bite, stir in 75ml boiling water, put the lid back on and simmer for a further 3–5 minutes | Stir in the roughly chopped coriander leaves and serve immediately with the roti

Pictured on pages 72–73

CURRY HOUSE JALFREZI

The spicy and flavourful jalfrezi has now overtaken tikka masala as Britain's favourite curry! This stock can be prepared in advance and frozen or kept in the fridge in an airtight container, so make a double batch to save time. Be sure to taste the curry as you go to get the perfect balance, as spices can vary in strength.

SERVES 3–4

1 large aubergine
4 tbsp sunflower or olive oil
1 onion
1 red pepper
a small bunch of fresh coriander
5 green bird's-eye chillies
12 cherry tomatoes
3 tbsp curry powder
1 tsp garam masala
¼–2 tsp hot chilli powder
8 tbsp tomato purée
500g cooked basmati rice, or use
    2 x 250g bags microwavable
    basmati rice, to serve
salt

FOR THE STOCK
1 onion
5cm piece fresh ginger
5 garlic cloves
500ml + 1 tbsp water
½ fresh red chilli
3 cherry tomatoes
1 tbsp sunflower or olive oil
¼ tsp ground coriander
¼ tsp ground cumin
¼ tsp ground fenugreek
¼ tsp ground turmeric
¼ tsp paprika

Preheat grill to 200°C | **Baking tray** | **Fine grater or Microplane** | **Medium saucepan** | **Liquidiser**

First cook the aubergine | Trim the aubergine and cut it into 2cm chunks | Spread over the baking tray | Sprinkle with 2 tablespoons oil and a good pinch of salt | Toss to coat | Grill for 15 minutes, turning occasionally | Remove when golden brown all over but not burnt

Meanwhile, make the stock | Peel and finely chop the onion | Peel the ginger by scraping off the skin with a spoon and grate | Peel and grate the garlic | Put the ginger and garlic into a bowl and mix with 1 tablespoon water to make a paste

Finely chop the red chilli and tomatoes | Place the saucepan on a medium heat and pour in the oil | Add the onion and sauté for 5 minutes | Add a teaspoon of the ginger and garlic paste | Add all the remaining spices and half the water and stir | Simmer for 10 minutes, until browned and reduced completely | Pour in the rest of the water, stir and transfer to the liquidiser | Blend to a smooth liquid | Clean out the pan

Back to the curry | Peel and thinly slice the onion | Cut the pepper in half and cut out the stem and seeds, then thinly slice | Pick the leaves from the coriander | Finely chop the stems and roughly chop the leaves | Trim and thinly slice two of the chillies | Quarter the tomatoes

Pour the remaining oil into the clean saucepan | Place over a high heat | Add the onion, pepper and sliced chillies and fry for 3 minutes, stirring regularly | Stir in the chopped coriander stems and remaining ginger and garlic paste (from making the stock) | Add the curry powder, garam masala, ¼ teaspoon hot chilli powder, tomato purée, grilled aubergines and stock | Taste and add more salt, garam masala and chilli powder if needed | Stir in the tomatoes | Simmer gently for 10 minutes, stirring frequently, until slightly thickened

Heat the rice or cook it following the instructions on the packet

Transfer to a serving dish | Cut the remaining chillies in half lengthways and use them to garnish the curry along with the chopped coriander leaves | Serve with the rice

ULTIMATE FALAFEL WRAP

Falafel has come to the rescue for us many times on a night out when we're a bit peckish, so we decided to recreate our own ultimate wrap for you guys to make at home. We recommend making your own hummus and chilli jam for but if you're feeling a bit lazy, feel free to use shop-bought ones instead.

SERVES 4

150g Chilli Jam (see page 79, or use 150g shop-bought)
1 x portion Falafels ingredients (see page 78)
1 x portion Hummus ingredients (see page 196, or use 400g shop-bought)
1 x portion Flatbreads (see page 78, or use 4 shop-bought)
50g fresh baby-leaf spinach or salad leaves
onion pickle, to serve (see page 107 or use any shop-bought pickle)
flat-leaf parsley, to garnish

Food processor | Large saucepan | Sterilised jars (see page 39) | Large frying pan | Line a large plate with kitchen paper | Cut 4 large squares of foil or parchment paper, about 32 x 32cm

Make the **Chilli Jam** first and leave it bubbling away while you prepare the rest of the meal | Clean out the food processor

Next, make the **Falafels** and set the first batch frying | Keep making them in batches until they are all cooked, transferring them to a baking tray with a tea towel over the top in the 50°C oven to keep warm while you finish other jobs | Clean the frying pan and food processor

Make your **Hummus**

Clean the work surface and dust it liberally with flour | Make and then cook the **Flatbreads**

Pick the flat-leaf parsley leaves, discard the stems and chop the leaves

Place a **Flatbread** on a square of foil or parchment paper | Spread a generous layer of **Hummus** over the flatbread | Dollop over big spoonfuls of Chilli Jam | Place 4 **Falafel Balls** in a line across the middle of the flatbread and squish them a little bit with your fingers | Top the line of falafel balls with a few fresh spinach or salad leaves, some onion pickle and flat-leaf parsley | Roll up the wrap tightly and secure the top and bottom with more foil or parchment paper

Tear open and eat

FALAFELS

MAKES 16

2 x 400g tins chickpeas
2 small red onions
3 garlic cloves
15g fresh coriander
15g fresh flat-leaf parsley
100g plain flour
2 tsp salt
1 tsp ground cumin
½ tsp black pepper
1½ tbsp harissa paste
½ lemon
olive oil, for frying

Food processor | Large frying pan | Line a large plate with kitchen paper

First get all your ingredients prepped | Drain the chickpeas, saving the water (aquafaba) for something else | Peel and roughly chop the red onions and garlic | Pick the leaves from the coriander and parsley, discard the stems and roughly chop

Now make the falafel mixture | Put all the ingredients except for the oil and lemon in the food processor | Squeeze in the lemon juice, catching any pips in your other hand | Blitz to a thick paste

Using wet hands, divide the batter into 16 and roll into balls about 3cm in diameter

Put the frying pan over a medium-high heat and add enough olive oil to cover the base of the pan | Once the oil is hot, carefully add the falafels and cook for 5–7 minutes, until golden all over and cooked through, turning regularly for even cooking (you may need to do this in batches) | Transfer to kitchen paper to drain before serving

3-INGREDIENT FLATBREADS

MAKES 4 THICK OR
8 THINNER FLATBREADS

500g plain flour, plus extra for dusting
1½ tsp salt
500g soya yoghurt

Clean work surface dusted liberally with flour | Large frying pan

To make the dough, put the flour and salt in a large mixing bowl and stir to combine | Make a well in the centre and spoon in the yoghurt | Combine with your hands to form a dough, making sure you incorporate all the flour | Tip onto the floured work surface and knead for a couple of minutes to bring the dough together (keep flouring the work surface and your hands to stop the dough sticking)

To make 4 thick flatbreads, divide the dough into 4 equal pieces and roll each one out to a circle 2–4mm thick and the size of a dinner plate (or just a little smaller than your biggest frying pan), adding more flour to the work surface as required | (To make 8 thinner ones, divide the dough into 8 and roll out to about a 1–2mm thickness)

Put the pan on a medium-high heat until hot | Carefully roll one of the flatbreads onto the rolling pin and transfer it to the frying pan | Cook for 2–3 minutes on each side | Repeat with the remaining flatbreads

CHILLI JAM

MAKES ABOUT 1.5kg

8 red peppers
12 fresh red chillies
1 scotch bonnet chilli, optional
5cm piece fresh ginger
8 garlic cloves
1 x 400g tin chopped tomatoes
750g golden caster sugar
250ml red wine vinegar

Food processor | Large saucepan | Sterilised jars (see page 39)

Start by getting your veg prepped | Cut the peppers in half and cut out the stems and seeds, then roughly chop | Rip the stems from the chillies, cut them in half lengthways and remove the seeds if you prefer a milder jam, then roughly chop | Peel the ginger by scraping off the skin with a spoon and roughly chop | Peel and roughly chop the garlic

Put the chopped ingredients into the food processor and pulse to finely chop

Tip the chopped vegetables into the saucepan and add all the rest of the ingredients | Put over a high heat and bring to the boil | Use a spoon to remove any scum that rises to the surface | Simmer for 70–90 minutes, stirring occasionally to prevent sticking, until really thick

Transfer to sterilised jars, put the lids on and leave to cool | Once opened, keep in the fridge and use within 1 month

HOLY TRINITY LOUISIANA GUMBO

We came back from one of our American trips with a real appetite for Southern comfort food and so gumbo had to make an appearance in this book. In this recipe we focus on the Holy Trinity of Cajun cooking: onions, bell peppers and celery. It's also a good one to freeze – defrost overnight in the fridge and then reheat on the stove until piping hot.

2 onions
2 celery sticks
2 green peppers
4 garlic cloves
300g okra
250g chestnut mushrooms
4 tomatoes
2 sprigs fresh thyme
4 tbsp olive oil
¼ tsp salt, plus a little extra
4 tbsp plain flour
1 tbsp tomato purée
1 tbsp apple cider vinegar
2 tsp smoked paprika
½ tsp cayenne pepper
1 tsp dried oregano
1 tsp Tabasco sauce
750ml vegetable stock
2 fresh bay leaves
240g tinned kidney beans
4 spring onions
500g cooked basmati rice, or use
    2 x 250g bags microwavable
    basmati rice, to serve
black pepper

Large casserole dish | Fine grater or Microplane

First get all your veg ready | Peel the onions | Trim the celery | Cut the peppers in half and cut out the stems and seeds | Roughly chop the onions, peppers and celery into small pieces | Peel and finely grate the garlic | Trim the okra and cut into 1cm-thick slices | Quarter the mushrooms | Finely chop the tomatoes | Roughly chop the thyme (if the stem is woody, remove the leaves by running your thumb and forefinger from the top to the base of the stem)

Put the casserole dish on a medium heat and pour in the oil | Once the dish is hot, add the onion, celery, peppers and ¼ teaspoon salt | Sweat for about 10 minutes, until softened | Add the garlic, okra and mushrooms and fry for a further 7–10 minutes, until the mushrooms are cooked through | Reduce the heat to medium-low, add the flour and stir to combine | Cook for another 5–7 minutes, stirring constantly to avoid burning, until golden brown (don't stop cooking too early, this browning is what gives your gumbo its rich colour)

Add the chopped tomatoes and tomato purée to the pan and stir for 2 minutes | Add the apple cider vinegar, thyme, smoked paprika, cayenne pepper, oregano and Tabasco and stir for 2 minutes | Pour in the vegetable stock | Add the bay leaves and kidney beans, reduce the heat to a very gentle simmer and cook for 30–35 minutes, until the broth is thick and hearty, stirring occasionally to make sure the bottom doesn't catch | Taste and season with salt and pepper

Heat the rice or cook it following the instructions on the packet

Trim and thinly slice the spring onions and sprinkle over the gumbo | Serve with the rice

TOFISH FINGER SANDWICH

A true shining star of a sandwich, this is our take on the classic British fish finger, combined with a quick tartare sauce and delightful mashy peas. Make more of the tartare sauce to keep in your fridge – it is great with our double-cooked chips on page 178 or a baked potato. The tofish fingers will keep really well in the freezer too.

MAKES 4

1 x 450g block extra-firm tofu
1 lemon
1 tsp salt
½ tsp black pepper
100ml white wine vinegar
1 tbsp Dijon mustard
100g plain flour
200ml unsweetened plant-based milk
100g golden breadcrumbs
olive oil, for frying
8 slices fresh crusty white bread
dairy-free butter, for spreading, optional
1 x portion Mashy Mashy Peas
    (see page 84)
1 x portion Speedy Tartare Sauce
    (see page 84)
tomato ketchup, optional

Tofu press or 2 clean tea towels and a weight such as a heavy book | Fine grater or Microplane | Large saucepan | Line 2 plates with kitchen paper

Press the tofu using a tofu press or place it between two clean tea towels, lay it on a plate and put a weight on top | Leave for at least 30 minutes to drain and firm up before you start cooking

Zest the lemon and squeeze the juice into the saucepan, catching the pips with your other hand | Add the zest, ½ teaspoon of the salt, the black pepper, white wine vinegar and mustard and mix | Drain any liquid from the tofu, cut it into 12 equal fingers and add them to the pan, turning to cover | Leave to marinate for 30 minutes

Meanwhile, make the batter | Pour the flour, remaining ½ teaspoon salt and the plant-based milk into a bowl and whisk to a batter | Put the breadcrumbs into another shallow bowl

Take the tofu fingers out of the marinade | Drop them into the batter and toss to coat completely | Transfer to the breadcrumbs and toss again, ensuring they are well covered | Place on a plate and set aside

Now get ready to cook the tofu | Quickly rinse the saucepan and pour in the olive oil until it's 2cm deep | Turn up the heat | Dip a wooden spoon into the oil and if bubbles form around the spoon, the oil is ready to cook | Carefully place the fingers in the oil and fry them in batches for 2–3 minutes, until golden and crispy all over | Transfer to the kitchen paper to soak up the excess oil

Build the sandwiches | Lay half the bread slices on plates and butter them if you prefer | Top with Speedy Tartare Sauce and ketchup, if using, the tofish fingers and Mashy Mashy Peas | Cut in half and serve

MASHY MASHY PEAS

SERVES 4

Kettle boiled | Stick blender, optional

200g frozen peas
1 tsp olive oil
1 tsp salt
1 tsp mint jelly or mint sauce

Pour the peas into a heatproof bowl, cover with boiling water and leave for 5 minutes to thaw

In another bowl, combine the olive oil, salt and mint jelly or sauce

Drain the peas, tip them into the mint mixture and stir through | Crush the peas with a fork or give them a quick blitz with a stick blender

SPEEDY TARTARE SAUCE

SERVES 4

100g egg-free mayonnaise
1 tbsp capers
1 small pickled gherkin
a pinch of salt
½ lemon

Put the dairy-free mayo into a small mixing bowl | Finely chop the capers and gherkins, add them to the bowl and stir everything together

Taste and season with the salt and lemon juice, catching any pips in your other hand as you squeeze the lemon half

GIANT BLT

These sandwiches are incredible. About half an hour after we posted this video on our channel a few BOSH! fans had already made it and sent us their pics! It's super-popular and we can see exactly why. Of course you can make this with regular-sized bread, but in true BOSH! style, we're making our sandwich big and bad. Why not take half to work with you?

SERVES 4

450g firm smoked tofu

25g cornflour

2 tbsp smoked paprika

1 tsp garlic powder

1 tsp smoked salt (or normal salt)

2 tbsp maple syrup, plus 1 tbsp for glazing

2 tbsp soy sauce

1 large ciabatta

1 baby gem lettuce

2 tomatoes

1 large avocado

6 tbsp egg-free mayonnaise

3 tbsp vegetable oil

2–3 tbsp red wine, for glazing

4 cornichons

salt and black pepper

Tofu press or 2 clean tea towels and a weight such as a heavy book | Deep-sided frying pan | Line a large plate with kitchen paper | 4 cocktail sticks

Press the tofu using a tofu press or place it between two clean tea towels, lay it on a plate and put a weight on top | Leave for at least 30 minutes to drain and firm up before you start cooking | Cut into 3mm-thick slices

Preheat the oven to 180°C

Make a coating for the tofu | Put the cornflour, smoked paprika, garlic powder and salt into a mixing bowl and mix together with a fork | Roll the tofu slices in the dry mix and transfer to a plate | Drizzle the 2 tablespoons maple syrup and soy sauce over the prepared tofu slices and set to one side

Put the bread in the oven and leave for 5–7 minutes to warm through | Meanwhile, separate the lettuce leaves | Trim and thinly slice the tomatoes | Halve and carefully stone the avocado by tapping the stone firmly with the heel of a knife so that it lodges in the stone, then twist and remove | Scoop out the flesh with a spoon and slice thinly | Take the bread out of the oven and slice it in half through the middle

Spread both halves of the ciabatta with a generous layer of egg-free mayo | Layer the slices of lettuce, tomato and avocado | Season with salt and pepper

Put the frying pan over a medium-high heat and pour in half the oil | When the pan is hot lay half the slices of tofu in the oil, then quickly but carefully add 1 tablespoon of red wine and ½ tablespoon of maple syrup | Toss the tofu in the glaze and fry until the liquid has evaporated and the tofu is well covered | Sprinkle over a small pinch of salt | Carefully turn the tofu slices over and sprinkle more salt on the other side | Fry until both sides are nice and browned, then transfer to the plate lined with kitchen paper to drain | Repeat to fry the remaining tofu, cleaning out the pan if necessary to prevent any residual maple syrup from burning

Lay the tofu bacon on top of the salad and put the lid on | Insert the cocktail sticks along the top of the sandwich and push the cornichons into the sticks | Cut into four equal pieces and serve immediately

SWEET POTATO TIKKA MASALA

The tikka masala was once Britain's best-loved curry, only recently overtaken by jalfrezi (see page 74). This recipe will give you a true curry house taste, with its super-thick and creamy sauce. Make a double or triple batch of the sauce and freeze it, or keep it in the fridge for up to 2 days, for a super-speedy curry in a hurry. It goes well with the rotis on page 70.

SERVES 4–6

700g sweet potatoes

3 tbsp vegetable oil

15g fresh coriander

1–2 fresh red chillies

2 red peppers

1 x 400ml tin full-fat coconut milk

hot chilli powder, optional

½ lemon

a handful of flaked almonds

500g cooked basmati rice, or use
    2 x 250g bags microwavable
    basmati rice, to serve, optional

rotis (shop-bought or see page 70),
    optional

salt and black pepper

FOR THE CURRY SAUCE

6cm piece fresh ginger

5 garlic cloves

1 onion

1½ fresh red chillies

4 cherry tomatoes

20g fresh coriander

1 tbsp vegetable oil

6 tbsp tomato purée

2 tbsp ground almonds

2 tsp garam masala

1 tsp ground coriander

1 tsp ground cumin

1 tsp smoked paprika

1 tsp salt

a pinch of ground fenugreek

a pinch of ground turmeric

500ml water

Preheat oven to 200°C | Line a baking tray | Fine grater or Microplane | Medium saucepan | Liquidiser

First roast the sweet potato | Peel the sweet potato and cut it into 2cm cubes | Put it on the baking tray, pour over 2 tablespoons of the oil, toss to coat and sprinkle with salt | Put into the hot oven for 20 minutes, turning occasionally, until soft and charring slightly at the edges | Remove and set aside

To make the curry sauce, peel the ginger by scraping off the skin with a spoon | Peel the garlic | Grate the ginger and garlic into a bowl and mix with a tablespoon of water | Peel and finely chop the onion | Finely chop the red chilli and tomatoes | Roughly chop the 20g coriander

Pour 1 tablespoon oil into the medium saucepan and place on a medium-high heat | Add the onion and sauté for 5 minutes | Add the ginger garlic paste and fry for 30 seconds | Add all the remaining curry sauce ingredients except for the water and stir | Pour in half the water, stir and simmer for 10 minutes, until browned and almost all the water has evaporated | Pour in the rest of the water, stir then pour everything into the liquidiser | Blend until smooth

Prepare the rest of the curry ingredients | Separate the leaves from the 15g fresh coriander and chop roughly, then finely chop the stems | Rip the stems from the fresh red chillies and chop finely | Cut the peppers in half, cut out the stems and seeds and chop into chunks

Splash 1 tablespoon oil into the same saucepan and place on a high heat | Add the chopped coriander stems, chilli and red pepper and fry for 3 minutes, until slightly softened | Pour in the curry sauce and coconut milk | Add the roasted sweet potato and stir | Taste and add more salt and hot chilli powder if you like it hot

Simmer for 10 minutes, until the sauce is nice and thick | Take off the heat and squeeze in the juice of half a lemon, catching any pips in your other hand | Taste and season to perfection

Heat the rice or cook it following the instructions on the packet

Plate up the tikka masala and garnish with the chopped coriander leaves and flaked almonds | Serve immediately

MINI MUSHROOM PIES

These little cheeky pies are a great party snack or they are great served on a plate with some mushy peas (see page 84) and chips (see page 178). If you want to save some time, prepare the filling a day in advance, then store it overnight in an airtight container in the fridge.

(see page 84) and chips (see page 178)

SERVES 12

1 onion
1 leek
1 garlic clove
750g chestnut mushrooms
2 sprigs fresh thyme
1 sprig fresh rosemary
3 tbsp olive oil, plus extra for greasing
2 x 320g sheets ready-rolled plant-based
    puff pastry
salt and black pepper

FOR THE BÉCHAMEL
2 tbsp olive oil
4 tbsp plain flour
350ml unsweetened plant-based milk

Preheat oven to 200°C | **Fine grater or Microplane** | **Large frying pan** | **Saucepan** | **Liquidiser or stick blender** | **Grease a 12-hole muffin tin with olive oil** | **8cm and 10cm round pastry cutters (or something else to use as a template)** | **Pastry brush**

Start by preparing the veg | Peel and finely chop the onion | Trim and thinly slice the leek | Peel and grate the garlic | Quarter the mushrooms | Remove the leaves from the herbs by running your thumb and forefinger from the top to the base of the stems (the leaves should easily come away) and finely chop

Put the frying pan over a medium heat | Add 2 tablespoons oil | Add the onion and a pinch of salt and cook for 3–5 minutes, stirring | Add the leek and stir for 7–8 minutes | Add the garlic and stir for 1 minute | Add the mushrooms, rosemary, thyme and 1 tablespoon oil and cook, stirring occasionally, for 10–12 minutes | Season to perfection | Increase the heat to high and cook for a further 10 minutes, until soft and all the liquid has evaporated | Remove from the heat and set aside

To make the béchamel, put the saucepan over a medium heat and add the oil | Add the flour and stir vigorously for 2–3 minutes | Gradually add the milk, whisking constantly until smooth | Bring to the boil, then simmer for 2 minutes, until thickened | Blend half the mushroom mixture with the stick blender or in a liquidiser until smooth | Add all the mushrooms to the pan and stir | Taste and season with salt and pepper

Unroll the pastry sheets and cut out twelve 10cm circles | Lightly press into the muffin holes so that there is some excess pastry peeping out from the tops | Divide the mushroom filling between the muffin holes | Cut out twelve 8cm circles, rerolling the pastry as necessary | Top the pies with the circles | Press the pastry circles together tightly to seal and crimp the edges with a fork | Brush with olive oil and put in the oven | Bake for 25–30 minutes, until golden and crispy | Take out of the oven and let the pies cool in the tin for a moment before serving

PULLED JACKFRUIT SANDWICH

This sandwich is simply incredible. It harks back to Henry's youth, working at a music website and eating pulled pork sandwiches for lunch. The jackfruit makes for an amazingly tasty filling, which combines perfectly with the carrot crackling and sweet applesauce to produce perhaps the best sandwich we've ever created.

MAKES 4

2 tbsp olive oil
1 tsp salt
½ tsp black pepper
½ tsp sugar
2 tsp dried sage
1½ tsp onion powder
1½ tsp garlic powder
½ tsp dried parsley
2 x 400g tins young green jackfruit
   in water or brine
8 tbsp cooked plant-based stuffing
   (shop-bought or make your own)
4 good-quality white bread rolls or
   English muffins
2 tbsp dairy-free butter
4 tbsp applesauce

FOR THE CARROT CRACKLING
1 medium carrot
1 tbsp olive oil
½ tsp salt
½ tsp smoked paprika

Preheat oven to 200°C | Line 2 baking trays

First roast the jackfruit | Add the olive oil, salt, pepper, sugar, sage, onion powder, garlic powder and parsley to a large bowl and mix together with a fork | Drain the jackfruit and fold it into the mixture | Spread the seasoned jackfruit over one of the baking trays, making sure it's well spaced out | Put the tray in the oven for 35–40 minutes, turning the jackfruit with tongs halfway through

If you're making your stuffing, follow the instructions on the packet

Meanwhile, make the carrot crackling | Peel or thinly slice the carrot into long slices | Put in a bowl, drizzle over the olive oil, sprinkle over the salt and smoked paprika and mix everything together to cover well | Spread on the second baking tray, making sure the slices are well spaced out | When the jackfruit has been in the oven for 15 minutes, add the tray of carrot slices to the oven and continue to cook both for 20 more minutes | Keep an eye on the carrots as they may not need the full 20 minutes – they will start to crisp and brown slightly, but make sure they don't blacken | Remove any pieces that look cooked and return the softer ones to the oven | Take the trays out of the oven

Cut the bread rolls in half and spread them with dairy-free butter | Spread applesauce over the bottom halves and top each one with 2 tablespoons of stuffing | Shred the jackfruit by pulling it apart with two forks and divide among the rolls | Finish with a generous helping of carrot crackling | Close the sandwiches and serve

BOSH! BANGERS WITH MASH & QUICK ONION GRAVY

This is a slightly fiddly recipe but the payoff is so worth it. These home-made sausages are so delicious, they make for an incredibly comforting dinner. But if you don't have time, use shop-bought sausages! We suggest doubling the recipe and freezing half the sausages, wrapped in foil and kept in an airtight container for up to a month. Defrost before cooking!

BOSH! BANGERS

MAKES 14 SMALL SAUSAGES
(AROUND 75g EACH)

2 carrots (about 300g)
1 parsnip (about 170g)
1 apple (about 150g)
5 garlic cloves
2 tbsp olive oil, plus more for greasing
1 onion
1 leek
a pinch of salt
25ml red wine
1 x 400g tin cannellini beans
a large bunch of thyme
a large bunch of rosemary
1 cooked beetroot (around 75g beetroot)
125g cooked brown basmati rice
100g vital wheat gluten
1 tsp Dijon mustard
¼ tsp black pepper
a pinch of chilli flakes

Preheat oven to 200°C | Line a baking tray | Large sauté pan or saucepan | Food processor | Cut out 14 pieces of foil to make 25 x 10cm rectangles | Steamer or large saucepan with a lid and a heatproof colander

. . . .

Start by roasting the root veg and apple | Peel and chop the carrots, parsnip and apple into 2cm pieces | Peel the garlic | Spread over the baking tray and drizzle with 1 tablespoon of the oil | Put the tray in the oven and cook for 25–30 minutes, until soft and slightly caramelised

Meanwhile, peel and thiny slice the onion and leek | Pour the rest of the oil into the large pan and put the pan over a medium heat | Add the onion and leek with a pinch of salt | Cook, stirring constantly, for 20–30 minutes, until the onions and leeks are dark and caramelised (caramelisation occurs on the base of the pan) | Pour in the red wine and use a wooden spoon to scrape the bottom of the pan | Once the wine has reduced slightly, tip the mixture into the bowl of a food processor, scraping in any bits from the bottom of the pan

Add the roasted vegetables and apple to the food processor | Drain the cannellini beans | Remove the leaves from the herbs by running your thumb and forefinger from the top to the base of the stems (the leaves should easily come away) | Add the leaves to the bowl along with all the remaining ingredients and the drained beans | Pulse until the mixture comes together to form a dough (don't overwork the dough, it will come together quite quickly and look like bright pink bread dough)

Boil the kettle | Pour the boiling water into the steamer or a large pan with a colander placed over the top

Brush the foil rectangles lightly with olive oil | Divide the sausage mixture between the foil pieces, putting about 75g in each one | Use your hands to roll them into sausage shapes and then wrap them in the foil, twisting tightly at each end to seal | Place the foil packages in the steamer or colander, put a lid on top and cook for 45 minutes (you may need to do this in batches)

Continued over the page

While the sausages are steaming, make the Incredible Mash, following the instructions below

Reheat the oven to 200°C | Re-line the baking tray

When the sausages have steamed, take them off the heat, allow them to cool a little and then carefully unwrap | Place on the lined baking tray and bake for 10 minutes, or until nice and browned

While the sausages are in the oven, make the Quick Onion Gravy (see opposite)

Spoon the smooth mash onto a serving plate or plates | Place the hot sausages on top | Pour onion gravy over the bangers and mash

INCREDIBLE MASH

SERVES 4

1kg King Edward or other floury potatoes
3 garlic cloves
5 tbsp good-quality extra-virgin olive oil
2 tbsp unsweetened plant-based milk
2–4 tsp mustard, optional
salt and black pepper

Large saucepan | Potato ricer, food mill or coarse sieve

Peel the potatoes and cut them into 3cm chunks | Place them in the pan along with the un-peeled garlic cloves and cover with water | Add a pinch of salt | Place over a high heat and bring to the boil | Cook for 15–17 minutes until tender | Drain well, remove the garlic cloves and return the potatoes to the dry pan for a few seconds to steam and dry

Mash the potatoes, using a potato ricer or food mill if you have one, spooning in the mashed potatoes and milling or ricing them into a large bowl or back into the pan | Alternatively, spoon the mash into a large coarse sieve and use a spatula or large spoon to force them through | Gradually stir the olive oil and plant-based milk into the potatoes | Season generously with salt and pepper | Add mustard, if using, stirring in a teaspoon at a time until you are happy with the flavour

QUICK ONION GRAVY

SERVES 4

2 red onions
1 tbsp olive oil
3 garlic cloves
3 sprigs fresh rosemary
1 tsp maple syrup
150ml red wine
4 tbsp warm water
1 heaped tbsp flour
2 tbsp balsamic vinegar
1 vegetable stock cube
350ml boiling water

Large saucepan on a medium heat | Fine grater or Microplane
| Kettle boiled

....

Peel and thinly slice the red onions | Add the olive oil to the pan | Once
the oil is hot, add the onions | Sauté for 7 minutes, stirring, until softened

Peel and grate the garlic and add to the pan | Cook for 1 minute

Meanwhile, remove the leaves from the rosemary by running your
thumb and forefinger from the top to the base of the stems (the leaves
should easily come away), finely chop and add to the pan | Add the
maple syrup and stir | Add the red wine | Increase the heat to medium,
stir everything together and let it bubble away for 8–10 minutes to
evaporate the alcohol

Put the warm water into a bowl or mug and add the flour | Stir with a
fork until all the lumps of flour are mixed in | Pour into the gravy | Add the
vinegar, stock cube and the boiling water | Bring to the boil, then reduce
the heat and simmer, stirring often, for 5–7 minutes, until thickened (the
gravy will thicken more as it cools)

ROAST SWEET POTATO TAGINE

Be whisked away to the Middle East with this hearty tagine. It's sweet, fragrant and easy to make. You can replace the preserved lemon with the grated zest of a lemon, the juice of half a lemon and an extra pinch of salt. It's also great with salad rather than the couscous for a lighter lunch.

SERVES 6

1kg sweet potatoes
3 tbsp olive oil
2 medium red onions
1 fresh red chilli
2 garlic cloves
6cm piece fresh ginger
30g fresh coriander
100g dried apricots
2 tbsp harissa paste
2 tsp ras el hanout
2 tsp ground cumin
2 tsp ground coriander
½ tsp sugar
2 x 400g tins chopped tomatoes
200ml water
1 x 240g tin chickpeas
salt and black pepper

FOR THE LEMON & ALMOND COUSCOUS
1 preserved lemon
1½ tbsp extra-virgin olive oil
1 tsp ground cumin
300g couscous
400ml boiling water
50g flaked almonds
20g fresh coriander leaves

Preheat oven to 180°C | Line a baking tray | Fine grater or Microplane | Large saucepan | Kettle boiled

First roast the sweet potato | Chop the sweet potatoes into 3cm chunks | Spread over the baking tray | Drizzle with 1 tablespoon of the olive oil and season with salt and pepper | Put in the oven and bake for 25 minutes

Meanwhile, peel and finely chop the red onions | Rip the stem from the chilli, cut it in half lengthways and remove the seeds, then finely chop | Peel and grate the garlic | Peel the ginger by scraping off the skin with a spoon and grate | Pluck the leaves from the coriander, put them to one side and thinly slice the stems | Roughly chop the dried apricots | Drain the chickpeas

To make the tagine, place the saucepan over a medium heat and add the rest of the olive oil | Add the onions and fry for 4–5 minutes, stirring, until starting to soften | Add the chilli, garlic, ginger and chopped coriander stems and stir for 2 minutes | Add the harissa paste, ras el hanout, cumin, ground coriander and sugar and stir for 1 minute | Add the chopped tomatoes and water | Lower the heat and simmer for 7–9 minutes | Stir in the drained chickpeas and apricots | Put the lid on and simmer for 8–10 minutes, stirring occasionally | Take the lid off the pan, taste and season | Add the coriander leaves and roasted sweet potato and stir | Reduce the heat to low and put the lid back on the pan

To make the couscous, halve the preserved lemon and put it into a mixing bowl | Add the olive oil, cumin, couscous and boiling water | Cover with a dinner plate and set aside for 8–10 minutes

Meanwhile, spread the flaked almonds over the baking tray | Put in the oven and bake for 4 minutes, until lightly browned | Finely chop the coriander leaves

Back to the couscous | Remove the preserved lemon and fluff the couscous with a fork | Reserve a quarter of the toasted almonds and a quarter of the chopped coriander leaves and fold the rest into the couscous | Taste and season with salt and pepper

Divide the couscous among bowls and top with the tagine | Garnish with the reserved almonds and coriander and serve

DOUGH 3-WAYS

This brilliantly versatile dough recipe can be used to make the pizzas, dough balls and flatbreads on the following pages. It's such an easy way to cook up some comfort food! Keep a batch of dough in the freezer, wrapped in cling film. Just remember to defrost it fully in the fridge before using.

MAKES ENOUGH FOR:
2 large pizzas (see page 102)
or 15 dough balls (see page 104)
or 4 flatbreads (see page 107)

500g strong white bread flour, plus
    a little extra
3.5g fast-action dried yeast
    (½ x 7g sachet)
1½ tsp salt
340ml water, at room temperature
vegetable oil or extra-virgin olive oil,
    for greasing

Clean work surface dusted liberally with flour | Cling film

Measure the flour into a large bowl | Stir in the yeast and salt and mix well | Use your hands to make a well in the middle of the flour | Pour in the water and slowly mix together, kneading well with your fingers | Add more flour if necessary so that it's not too sticky

When the dough has come together, take it out of the bowl and put it on the floured work surface | Knead for 15 minutes, stretching and folding the dough, turning it 90 degrees then repeating until it becomes really smooth and springy

Prove the dough | Wipe any flour or dough out of the bowl and rub the inside lightly with oil | Put the dough back in, cover the bowl with cling film and leave to rise for about 1 hour, until doubled in size | This is the first prove and your dough is now ready to make into one of the following recipes

MARGHERITA PIZZA

Pizza has a special place in our hearts, and when we are feeling adventurous we'll top ours with a home-made cashew mozzarella. You can of course use a shop-bought dairy-free cheese, but if you have the time, this one is excellent. The mozzarella will keep for a couple of days in the fridge. And, of course, this is pizza, so play around with your favourite toppings!

MAKES 2 LARGE PIZZAS

1 x portion basic dough (see page 101)
20 fresh basil leaves, to garnish
semolina, for dusting

FOR THE MOZZARELLA
250g cashews
300ml aquafaba (the drained water
    from 2–3 x 400g tins chickpeas)
3 tbsp coconut oil
5 tbsp tapioca flour
2 tbsp nutritional yeast
1 tsp salt
½ lemon

FOR THE TOMATO SAUCE
1 x 400g tin chopped tomatoes
1 garlic clove
5g fresh basil leaves
2 tsp dried oregano
½ tsp caster sugar
a pinch of salt
a pinch of black pepper
1 tbsp olive oil
1 tbsp balsamic vinegar

Clean work surface dusted liberally with flour | **Cling film** | **Medium saucepan of hot water on a high heat** | **Liquidiser** | **Pizza stone or heavy baking sheet** | **Large baking sheet dusted with semolina** | **Rolling pin or clean, dry wine bottle**

Tip the basic dough on to the floured work surface | Knead for 1 minute to knock it back, then divide it in two | Cover each half with cling film and leave to prove for another 30 minutes

Meanwhile, make the mozzarella | Put the cashews in the pan of hot water and boil for 15 minutes, until they are soft and have rehydrated (alternatively, soak in cold water for at least 2 hours or ideally overnight)

Drain the cashews then put all the ingredients for the mozzarella except for the lemon into the liquidiser | Squeeze over the lemon juice, catching the pips in your other hand | Blend to a smooth cream, then pour into the saucepan | Put the pan over a medium heat and stir for 10–15 minutes, until the mixture is thick and gloopy | Transfer to a plate and form into a rough oblong shape with your hands | Leave to cool | Cut into about 8 equal pieces and shape into balls | Transfer to the fridge

Preheat the oven to 250°C | Put the pizza stone or heavy baking sheet on the middle shelf of the oven to heat up | Clean out the liquidiser | Dust the work surface with more flour

Add all the tomato sauce ingredients to the liquidiser and blend to a smooth paste | Taste and season | Pour the sauce into the saucepan and simmer for 15 minutes, until thick

Roll one dough half out to make a pizza base about 30cm wide | Carefully roll it back on to the rolling pin and transfer to the baking sheet dusted with semolina | Spread over half the tomato sauce, leaving a 2.5cm rim around the edge

Take the mozzarella out of the fridge and slice the balls in half | Place half the slices over the pizza | Slide on to the hot pizza stone or baking sheet in the oven and bake for 10–12 minutes, until the crust has bubbled up and begun to darken | Prepare the second pizza

Slide the cooked pizza on to a wooden board or plate | Put the second pizza in to cook | Garnish the cooked pizzas with basil leaves and serve

CHEESEBURGER DOUGH BALLS

These little bites of heaven are amazing and taste just like the real thing. They were a smash hit on our social media channels so we decided to bring them to life in this book! We recommend making double and freezing some for later. Simply pop them in an airtight container in the freezer instead of cooking them. Cook from frozen for 40–45 minutes.

MAKES 15

6 plant-based sausages
1 tsp garlic powder
1 tbsp Dijon mustard
½ tsp salt
½ tsp black pepper
olive oil, for drizzling and brushing
8 slices dairy-free cheese
1 x portion basic dough (see page 101)
8 tsp red onion chutney
black sesame seeds, for sprinkling
ketchup, for dunking

Preheat oven to 180°C | Line a baking tray | Microwavable plate, optional | Clean work surface dusted liberally with flour | Rolling pin or clean, dry wine bottle | Line a baking sheet with parchment paper | Pastry brush

First make the filling | Put the sausages on a microwavable plate | If they are frozen, cook on high for 90 seconds, if they're not frozen, cook for 20 seconds | Take the sausages out of the microwave and mash them with a fork to get them gooey and malleable | Alternatively, defrost the sausages in the fridge overnight, put them in the oven for 7 minutes and mash with a fork

Transfer the mashed sausage to a bowl and add the garlic powder, mustard, salt and pepper and mix | Divide into 15 equal portions and roll into balls | Place the balls on the baking tray and flatten them into mini burger patties that are about 4cm wide and 2cm high | Drizzle with olive oil | Put the tray in the oven and bake for 10–12 minutes, until the patties are golden | Take the tray out of the oven and lay it on a heatproof surface

Meanwhile, cut the slices of dairy-free cheese into quarters

Tip the dough on to the floured work surface and knead for 1 minute to knock it back | Cut it into 15 equal portions and roll into balls | Roll each ball out to circles 5mm thick | Place a slice of cheese in the centre of each circle | Put ½ teaspoon red onion chutney on top of each slice of cheese and top with a mini burger | Top with another slice of cheese | Carefully fold up the edges of the dough circles around the burgers, pinching the tops to neatly seal them

Flip over the dough balls and lay them sealed side down on the lined baking sheet | Brush liberally with olive oil and sprinkle with sesame seeds, gently pressing the seeds into the dough | Put the tray in the oven and bake for 25–30 minutes, until golden brown

Remove from the oven, transfer to a plate and serve with tomato ketchup to dunk in

KEBABISH TANDOORI SPECIAL

A kebab done well is a glorious thing, and though they often get a bad rep, when they're filled with veggies they can be incredibly healthy. These tandoori cauliflower chunks taste gorgeous – the combination of flavours inside one of these wraps is incredible. To save time on the day you can marinate your cauliflower florets overnight.

MAKES 4

1 head cauliflower (about 650g)
15g fresh mint
½ cucumber
4 tomatoes
1 x portion Basic Dough (see page 101)
chilli sauce (shop-bought or
    see page 161)

FOR THE TANDOORI MARINADE
3 garlic cloves
5cm piece fresh ginger
200g coconut yoghurt
2 tbsp vegetable oil
2 tsp garam masala
1 tsp smoked paprika
1 tsp ground turmeric
1 tsp ground cumin
1 tsp ground coriander
¾ tsp salt
½ tsp chilli powder

FOR THE MINT RAITA
200g plant-based yoghurt
½ tsp sugar
½ tsp salt
2 tsp mint sauce
⅛ tsp cayenne pepper
½ lemon

FOR THE QUICK RED ONION PICKLE
1 garlic clove
½ tsp sugar
½ tsp salt
100ml clear vinegar
    (e.g. white wine or rice)
1 medium red onion

Preheat oven to 200°C | Line a large baking tray and lay a metal cooling rack on top | Sieve or colander | Kettle boiled | Fine grater or Microplane | Clean work surface dusted liberally with flour | Large frying pan | Rolling pin or clean, dry wine bottle | Cut out four 30 x 30cm squares of foil or parchment paper

. . . .

First make the pickle | Peel the garlic, cut it in half and put it in a bowl | Add the sugar, salt and vinegar and stir to dissolve | Peel and thinly slice the onion and put the slices in a colander over the sink | Pour over boiling water | Drain and add to the bowl | Stir to mix and set aside

Now make the marinade | Peel and grate the garlic | Peel the ginger then finely grate it | Put all the marinade ingredients into a large bowl and mix together | Taste and adjust the seasoning if necessary

Trim the cauliflower and break into 3cm florets | Add to the marinade and mix well | Transfer the cauliflower to the cooling rack | Put the tray in the oven and bake for 25–30 minutes, until the cauliflower is darkening and getting crispy

Meanwhile, make the raita by putting the yoghurt, sugar, salt, mint sauce and cayenne into a bowl | Squeeze in the juice of the lemon, catching any pips | Mix, taste and adjust the seasoning if necessary

Pick the leaves from the coriander and discard the stems | Coarsely chop the cucumber and tomatoes

Tip the risen basic dough on to the floured work surface and knead for 1 minute | Cut the dough in half and use one half for something else | Cut the rest into 4 equal pieces | Place the frying pan over a medium-high heat | Roll out one piece of dough until it is 25cm wide and very thin, dusting with flour as you go | Once the pan is really hot, carefully lay the flatbread in the pan | Cook until light brown marks and bubbles appear on the bottom of the bread, 2–3 minutes | Flip and repeat | Transfer to a plate and leave to cool | Repeat to make all the breads

Lay out the foil or paper squares and place a flatbread on each | Spoon the raita, cucumber, tomatoes and cauliflower down the middles | Add spoonfuls of onion pickle and sprinkle over the mint | Finish with a good helping of chilli sauce and roll the kebabs tightly in the foil or paper | Rip open to enjoy

SHEPHERD'S PIE

This is perhaps one of Ian's favourite dishes: the British classic, shepherd's pie. Served with garden peas it is perfect for a cold winter evening. You can prepare the filling and mash the day before and keep them in separate airtight containers in the fridge, then assemble the pie when you're ready to cook it. It might take a few minutes longer if you're cooking it from cold.

SERVES 4–6

2 medium red onions
1 celery stick
3 garlic cloves
4 sun-dried tomatoes,
    plus 2 tbsp oil from the jar
1 sprig fresh rosemary
3 sprigs fresh thyme
1 large carrot
500g mushrooms
2 tbsp tomato purée
1 tbsp yeast extract (e.g. Marmite)
1 tbsp balsamic vinegar
250ml red wine
100ml vegetable stock
400g pre-cooked puy lentils
salt and black pepper

FOR THE POTATO TOPPING

1.2kg Maris Piper or other floury
    potatoes
40g dairy-free butter
150ml unsweetened plant-based milk
1 tbsp Dijon mustard

Preheat oven to 180°C | Fine grater or Microplane | 2 large saucepans | Food processor | Potato masher | 20 x 30cm lasagne dish | Piping bag fitted with a wide star nozzle, optional

First make a start on the potato topping | Peel and chop the potatoes into large chunks | Put in a saucepan, cover with cold water and add a generous pinch of salt | Put over a high heat, bring to the boil and cook for 12–15 minutes | Drain into a colander and leave to dry | Tip back into the pan

Now to the filling | Peel and finely dice the red onions and celery | Peel and grate the garlic | Finely chop the sun-dried tomatoes | Remove the leaves from the rosemary and thyme by running your thumb and forefinger from the top to the base of the stems (the leaves should easily come away), then finely chop | Peel and finely chop the carrot | Put the mushrooms in the food processor and blitz to mince

Put the second saucepan over a medium heat | Pour in the sun-dried tomato oil | Add the onion and a small pinch of salt | Fry for 5 minutes, stirring | Add the garlic, sun-dried tomatoes, rosemary and thyme and cook for 2 minutes | Add the carrot and celery and stir for 4–5 minutes | Add the mushrooms, turn up the heat slightly and stir for 2–3 minutes, until the mushrooms start to sweat | Reduce the heat and cook for 5–7 minutes, stirring occasionally

Stir the tomato purée into the pan | Add the yeast extract and balsamic vinegar and stir for 1 minute | Add the red wine, stock and lentils, turn up the heat and simmer until most of the liquid has evaporated, about 10 minutes | Taste, season and take off the heat

Mash the potatoes | Add the dairy-free butter, milk and mustard to the potatoes and mash until really smooth | Taste and season

Spread the filling over the bottom of the lasagne dish | Spoon the potato into the piping bag, if using, and pipe tightly packed walnut-sized whips of potato all over, otherwise spoon over the potato and spread it out with the back of a spoon, then drag over a fork to make rows that will catch and brown in the oven

Put the pie in the oven and bake for 25–30 minutes, until starting to crisp and turn golden brown | Remove and serve

3

FEASTS

Henry's favourite
Easy Peasy Roast Dinner

Ian's favourite
Classic Lasagne

CLASSIC LASAGNE

Lasagne will always be one of our favourites, and this simple mushroom ragu with a rich, creamy béchamel is a real classic. We don't think you should mess with perfection, but you could add a few chilli flakes if you like. The ragu and béchamel can be made the day before and kept in the fridge, so on the day you just have to build and bake the final dish.

SERVES 6–8

2 onions
100g sun-dried tomatoes, plus 2 tbsp
   oil from the jar
3 carrots
3 celery sticks
1 sprig fresh rosemary, plus more
   for garnish
2 sprigs fresh thyme
4 garlic cloves
700g chestnut mushrooms
300ml red wine
1 tbsp tomato purée
1 tbsp red miso paste
1 tsp balsamic vinegar
½ tsp dried oregano
2 tsp soy sauce
2 x 400g tins chopped plum tomatoes
800ml water
500g dried lasagne sheets
salt and black pepper
salad leaves, to serve

FOR THE BÉCHAMEL
125ml olive oil
125g flour
1.25 litres unsweetened plant-based milk
1½ tbsp nutritional yeast

Food processor | 2 large saucepans, one on a medium heat | Fine grater or Microplane | 25 x 30cm lasagne dish | Foil

Peel and quarter the onions and blitz them in the food processor until finely chopped | Add the sun-dried tomato oil to the large pan on the heat and sauté the onions, stirring, for 5–6 minutes

Meanwhile, peel the carrots and pulse them in the food processor with the celery until minced | Remove the leaves from the rosemary and thyme and finely chop | Peel and grate the garlic and add it to the pan | Stir for 1 minute | Add the carrot, celery, rosemary and thyme, reduce the heat slightly and sauté, stirring occasionally, for 12–15 minutes

Meanwhile, thinly slice the sun-dried tomatoes | Pulse the mushrooms in the food processor until finely minced | Add to the pan along with the sun-dried tomatoes | Stir, increase the heat slightly and sauté, stirring, for 8–10 minutes

Pour in the wine, increase the heat and stir constantly for 5–6 minutes, until nearly all the liquid has evaporated | Add the tomato purée, miso paste, balsamic vinegar, oregano and soy sauce and stir for 1 minute | Add the chopped tomatoes and water | Lower the heat to medium and simmer for 30 minutes | Taste and season

While it is simmering, make the béchamel | Put the second pan over a medium heat and add the olive oil | Add the flour and stir for 3–5 minutes | Gradually add the milk, stirring constantly | Add the nutritional yeast and stir until smooth | Bring to the boil then lower the heat and simmer until the béchamel thickens to the consistency of custard | Taste and season | Preheat the oven to 180°C

Now, layer up your lasagne | Spread a quarter of the ragu into the lasagne dish | Spoon over a quarter of the béchamel | Cover with lasagne sheets, breaking them if necessary to make a complete layer with no gaps | Repeat three times, reserving some béchamel to cover the top completely | Garnish with a few rosemary leaves | Cover with foil and put on the lowest shelf of the oven | Bake for 50 minutes | Remove the foil and bake for a further 15 minutes | Leave to stand for 10 minutes before serving with the salad leaves | The leftovers will taste amazing the next day – simply bring back to piping hot in the oven or microwave

SEASIDE ROLL WITH SALSA VERDE & NEW POTATOES

This seaside roll is our plant-based take on a salmon en croute and is a beautiful, exciting centrepiece. The salsa verde gives a fresh zing to the new potatoes and is the perfect side sauce for the crispy seaside roll. Pressing your tofu is really important here as we don't want the pastry to become soggy.

1 x 400g block firm tofu
3 garlic cloves
1 lemon
4cm piece fresh ginger
3 roasted red peppers from a jar
1 tbsp olive oil, plus more for glazing
1 tsp salt, plus extra to season
½ large cucumber
2 spring onions
15g fresh dill
1 tbsp Dijon mustard
½ tbsp white wine vinegar
1 tsp light agave nectar
50g watercress, plus extra to serve
1 x 340g sheet ready-rolled plant-based
   puff pastry
unsweetened plant-based milk, for
   brushing
black pepper

FOR THE SALSA VERDE
30g fresh parsley
30g fresh mint
2 small garlic cloves
3 tbsp capers
1 large pickled gherkin
1 tbsp Dijon mustard
3 tbsp red wine vinegar
150–180ml extra-virgin olive oil
salt and black pepper

FOR THE NEW POTATOES
1.2kg new potatoes
a large pinch of salt
10g fresh parsley leaves
10g fresh dill leaves
3 tbsp olive oil
salt and black pepper

Tofu press or 2 clean tea towels and a weight such as a heavy book
| Fine grater or Microplane | Food processor | Baking sheet | Large saucepan

Press the tofu using a tofu press or place it between two clean tea towels, lay it on a plate and put a weight on top | Leave for at least an hour to drain and firm up | Preheat oven to 180°C

Make the tofu filling | Peel the garlic | Zest and juice the lemon | Peel and grate the ginger | Put the roasted red peppers, tofu, oil, garlic, lemon juice and zest, ginger and 1 teaspoon salt into the food processor and pulse until combined | Season with salt and pepper

Prepare the cucumber filling | Cut the cucumber in half lengthways, scrape out the seeds and cut into 1cm-thick slices | Thinly slice the spring onions | Finely chop the dill | Place the cucumber, spring onions, mustard, white wine vinegar, agave nectar, dill and watercress in a bowl, season with salt and pepper and set aside

Unroll the pastry and lay it on its paper on the baking sheet | Spread half the tofu mixture neatly, lengthways, down one side of the pastry, leaving a 2cm border | Cover the tofu with the cucumber mixture and then another layer of tofu | Neaten the filling so that it's firm and smooth | Brush the edges of the pastry with plant-based milk | Gently pull the exposed pastry up and over the filling | Press along the edge to seal, then crimp with a fork | Using a sharp knife make a cross-hatch pattern across the top, as well as a few slits | Brush with olive oil | Put the baking sheet in the oven for 35–40 minutes, until golden and crispy | Remove from the oven

Meanwhile, make the salsa verde | Clean out the food processor | Separate the herb leaves and discard the stems | Put the leaves in the food processor | Peel the garlic and add to the herbs with the capers and gherkin | Pulse to finely chop | Remove the blade | Add the mustard and vinegar and mix well | Gradually stir in the oil until you reach your desired consistency | Taste and season

Put the new potatoes in the large saucepan, cover with cold water and sprinkle over the salt | Put on a high heat and boil for 10–12 minutes, until tender | Roughly chop the parsley and dill leaves | Drain the potatoes and tip them back into the pan | Drizzle over the olive oil | Sprinkle over the herbs | Season and toss to coat

Slice the Seaside Roll | Serve with potatoes, salsa verde and watercress

PAN-FRIED SEITAN STEAK WITH SECRET SAUCE

This steak is succulent and satisfying and the secret sauce is out of this world! You'll impress all of your carnivore friends. Serve with our Double-Cooked Rosemary Chips (see page 178) and a side salad for the perfect fancy dinner. For a drier, firmer texture press the steak as you would tofu – wrapping it in kitchen paper and placing a weight on top for 20 minutes.

SERVES 4

180g vital wheat gluten
75g pre-cooked puy lentils
2 tbsp nutritional yeast
2 tbsp tomato purée
1 tbsp garlic powder
1 tbsp chilli powder
1 tbsp soy sauce
½ tsp smoked salt
½ tsp black pepper
90ml water
a splash of oil
150g chips per person, to serve

FOR THE MARINADE
2 tbsp olive oil
1 tbsp soy sauce
1 tbsp maple syrup

Food processor | Clean work surface | Large saucepan of salted water on a high heat | Large freezer bag | Sauté pan

First make the steak | Add all the ingredients, apart from the water and oil, to the food processor and pulse to combine | Add the water and blitz, scraping down the sides as needed | Tip the mixture on to a clean work surface, knead for a minute or two then bring it together into a tight ball

Roll the mixture into a rough oblong shape and cut into 4 even slices | Flatten each slice with your hand so they're roughly 1cm thick and steak-shaped (you can also use a rolling pin here) | For a dryer texture press the steak as you would tofu – wrapping it in kitchen paper and placing a weight on top of it for 20 minutes, which will give a firmer texture

Lower the steaks into the pan of boiling salted water and simmer for 25 minutes | Take the steaks out of the pan, drain and leave to cool for 5 minutes

Put the ingredients for the marinade into a large freezer bag | Put the steaks in the bag and roll them around in the marinade so they are well coated | Leave to marinate for 20 minutes | While the steaks are marinating, make the Café de Paris Secret Sauce (see opposite)

When you're ready to cook the steaks place a sauté pan over a medium-high heat | Add a splash of oil and let it get hot | Add the steaks and pour over any remaining marinade | Cook for 2–3 minutes on each side, basting the steaks with the oil in the pan as they cook | Remove when both sides are well browned, but the steak is still tender | Leave to rest for a couple of minutes before serving with chips and Secret Sauce poured over in true Café de Paris style

Pictured on pages 118–119

CAFÉ DE PARIS SECRET SAUCE

MAKES ABOUT 300ml

Saucepan | Liquidiser

2 large eschalion (banana) shallots
3 garlic cloves
20g fresh tarragon
1 tsp capers
1½ tbsp olive oil
500ml vegetable stock
60ml white wine
3 tbsp red wine vinegar
2 tbsp Dijon mustard
1 tsp soy sauce
1 tsp black pepper
1 tsp salt

Prep the ingredients | Peel and thinly slice the shallots | Peel and finely chop the garlic | Pick the tarragon leaves, discard the stems, then finely chop | Finely chop the capers

Put the saucepan over a medium heat | Add 1 tablespoon of the olive oil | Add the garlic and shallots and cook for 4–5 minutes until soft, stirring occasionally | Add the vegetable stock and simmer for 3–4 minutes | Add all the remaining ingredients and bring to the boil, then simmer for 10 minutes until the sauce has reduced a little and become thicker | Take the pan off the heat and set aside to cool to room temperature

Pour the sauce into the liquidiser and blend until smooth | Pour back into the pan and bring to a simmer | Stir through the remaining ½ tablespoon olive oil before serving

HENRY'S BIRYANI WITH CORIANDER CHUTNEY

This dish is a revelation. Jackfruit is a traditional Indian ingredient and it does an incredible job of soaking up the aromatic spices. You can use whatever vegetables you like though – 800g sweet potatoes, pumpkin or any mix of veg would be perfect. Simply boil or roast until softened but still a little firm, then use them in place of the jackfruit.

SERVES 6

200g basmati rice
500ml boiling water
10 green cardamom pods
7 garlic cloves
3 fresh bay leaves
3 cinnamon sticks
2 x 400g tins young green jackfruit
    in water or brine
2 onions
3cm piece fresh ginger
¼ tsp black peppercorns
8 tbsp vegetable oil
1 tsp red chilli powder
2 tsp ground coriander
1 tsp ground cumin
1 tsp ground turmeric
120g dairy-free yoghurt
1 x portion Coriander Chutney
    ingredients (see page 122)
1 x portion Mint Raita
    (see page 107), optional
salt

Preheat oven to 180°C | Kettle boiled | Small saucepan with a tight-fitting lid on a medium heat | Sauté pan | Line a plate with kitchen paper | Small roasting tin | Foil

First cook the rice | Rinse the rice under cold running water until the water runs clear | Drain and tip into the saucepan | Pour over 400ml of the boiling water | Add a pinch of salt, 6 of the cardamom pods, 4 garlic cloves, 2 bay leaves and 2 cinnamon sticks | Turn up the heat and bring to the boil, stir once, then reduce the heat to the lowest setting | Put the lid on and cook for 6 minutes | Don't touch the rice until the time is up | Take the pan off the heat, drain the rice in a sieve, then tip it back into the pan and put the lid on

Drain the jackfruit | Peel and thinly slice the onions and remaining 3 garlic cloves | Peel the ginger by scraping off the skin with a spoon and chop finely | Crush the remaining cardamom pods and the peppercorns

Place the sauté pan over a high heat and add 4 tablespoons of the oil | Add the onions to the hot pan, sprinkle over a pinch of salt and fry, stirring constantly, for 10 minutes, until the onions are dark and crispy, but not burnt | Transfer to the kitchen paper

Add 2 tablespoons more oil to the pan | Add the remaining 1 bay leaf, the sliced garlic cloves, cinnamon stick, crushed cardamom and peppercorns and fry for 2 minutes | Add the jackfruit and roughly pull the strands apart with a fork | Fry for 2 minutes, stirring continuously | Add the ginger, chilli powder, ground coriander, cumin and turmeric and fry for 5 minutes more | Taste and season | Add the yoghurt and 100ml boiling water to the pan | Lower the heat to medium and stir for 2–3 minutes | Taste and season then remove from the heat

Continued over the page

Spoon a layer of rice over the base of the roasting tin | Add a layer of jackfruit | Sprinkle over a spoonful of the onions | Repeat this layering to use up all the ingredients, finishing with a layer of rice, with some jackfruit and onion peeping through | Drizzle the remaining oil over the biryani, cover with foil and put the tin in the oven | Bake for 20–25 minutes

While the biryani is baking, make your Coriander Chutney, following the instructions below

Take the tin out of the oven and remove the foil | Spoon the biryani into bowls or plates, drizzle over the Coriander Chutney and serve immediately with some raita on the side

CORIANDER CHUTNEY

MAKES ABOUT 120g

Liquidiser

4 spring onions
2cm piece fresh ginger
1 small fresh red chilli
30g fresh coriander
10g fresh mint leaves
¾ tsp salt
½ tsp sugar
½ tsp garam masala
¼ tsp cayenne pepper
2 tbsp vegetable oil
1 tbsp water
1 lemon

First get your ingredients ready | Trim and roughly chop the spring onions | Peel the ginger by scraping off the skin with a spoon and chop roughly | Rip the stem from the chilli

Put all the ingredients except for the lemon in the liquidiser | Zest the lemon into the liquidiser and then cut it in half and squeeze in the juice, catching any pips with your other hand | Blend everything together and then check the consistency, adding more water if it's too thick | Transfer to a bowl and serve | This chutney is also great with poppadoms

EASY PEASY ROAST DINNER

This is such a good roast dinner, with the awesome jackfruit taking centre stage. It takes a little while, but most of the time it's your oven that's doing all the hard work! The process for making the jackfruit is similar to the jackfruit sandwich on page 92, so you could double up on this one and have leftovers for delicious jack and carrot crackling sandwiches the next day!

SERVES 4

1 x portion Herb Oil ingredients (see page 127)

1 x portion Roasted Root Vegetables ingredients (see page 126)

1 x portion Pulled Jackfruit ingredients (see page 126)

1 x portion Quick Red Wine Gravy ingredients (see page 127)

170g shop-bought plant-based stuffing

small jar shop-bought applesauce

Preheat oven to 200°C | Line 1 baking tray | 1 large saucepan with a lid | Colander | Kettle boiled | Liquidiser | Roasting tin

....

Make your **Herb Oil** following the instructions on page 127

Then get your **Roasted Root Vegetables** in the oven on the top shelf, following the instructions on page 126

Next, make your **Pulled Jackfruit** and get that in the oven on the middle shelf, following the instructions on page 126

Next, prepare your stuffing following the instructions on the packet | Put in the oven on the bottom shelf

While they're all roasting, make your **Red Wine Gravy**, following the instructions on page 127

Serve piping hot with the applesauce on the side

Pictured on pages 124–125

PULLED JACKFRUIT

SERVES 4

3 x 400g tins young green jackfruit
   in water or brine
5 tbsp Herb Oil (see opposite) or olive oil
½ tsp salt
1 tsp black pepper
1 tsp sugar
4 tsp dried sage
3 tsp onion powder
3 tsp garlic powder
½ tsp smoked paprika
1 tsp dried parsley

Preheat oven to 200°C | Line a baking tray | Clean tea towel or kitchen paper

Drain the jackfruit, rinse under a cold tap and pat dry with a clean tea towel or kitchen paper

Put all the ingredients except for the jackfruit into a large mixing bowl and mix with a fork | Add the jackfruit and toss to coat it in the seasoning

Spread out the seasoned jackfruit on the baking tray, making sure the pieces are well spaced out | Put the tray in the oven to cook for 35−40 minutes, or until very lightly charred and crispy, turning the jackfruit halfway through | Remove from the oven, transfer to a bowl and serve immediately

ROASTED ROOT VEGETABLES

SERVES 4

900g Maris Piper or other floury
   potatoes
5−6 carrots (about 500g)
3−4 parsnips (about 500g)
4 eschalion (banana) shallots
1 garlic bulb
120ml Herb Oil (see opposite) or olive oil
4 sprigs fresh rosemary
8 sprigs fresh thyme
salt and black pepper

Preheat oven to 200°C | Large roasting tin | Large saucepan

Peel the vegetables | Cut the potatoes into quarters | Cut the carrots and parsnips into 3cm chunks | Peel and quarter the shallots | Break the garlic bulb into individual cloves, but don't peel them

Pour the oil into the roasting tin, put the tin in the oven and leave it to heat up for 10 minutes

Meanwhile, add the potatoes and carrots to the saucepan, cover with cold water and throw in a generous pinch of salt | Put the pan on a high heat, bring to the boil and cook for 4 minutes | Add the parsnips and cook for a further 4 minutes | Tip the veggies into a colander, tossing them around to rough up the edges | Set aside

Take the tin out of the oven and set it down on a heatproof surface | Carefully spoon the veggies into the tin and roll them around in the hot oil to make sure they're well coated | Sprinkle over the shallots, garlic cloves, rosemary and thyme and season with salt and pepper | Put the tin in the oven to roast for about 1 hour, stirring every 20 minutes to ensure an even, crispy cook | Remove from the oven and serve

HERB OIL

MAKES ABOUT 500ml

Liquidiser | Sterilised bottle (see page 39)

4 sprigs fresh rosemary
8 sprigs fresh thyme
1 tsp salt
½ tsp black pepper
500ml groundnut or rapeseed oil

Remove the leaves from the herbs by running your thumb and forefinger from the top to the base of the stems (the leaves should easily come away) then finely chop | Put all the ingredients into the liquidiser | Blend until smooth and then leave to rest for 10 minutes | Pour through a sieve into a measuring jug | Use immediately or pour into the bottle and refrigerate | Use within a week

RED WINE GRAVY

MAKES ABOUT 600ml

Fine grater or Microplane | Medium saucepan | Large heatproof bowl with a sieve on top

2 red onions
3 garlic cloves
2 carrots
2 celery sticks
2 tbsp Herb Oil (see above) or olive oil
1 sprig fresh rosemary
2 sprigs fresh thyme
250ml red wine
1 tbsp tomato purée
1 tsp yeast extract (e.g. Marmite)
1 tsp mustard
1 litre vegetable stock (preferably liquid
    stock from sachets)
2 tbsp water
3 tbsp plain flour
salt and black pepper

First prep the veg | Peel and roughly chop the red onions | Peel and finely grate the garlic | Peel and coarsely grate the carrots | Thinly slice the celery

Put the saucepan on a medium-low heat and add the oil | Add the onions to the hot pan and fry for 5 minutes, stirring, until starting to soften | Add the garlic and stir for 1 minute | Add the carrot and celery and fry for 15–17 minutes, stirring every minute to ensure nothing sticks to the pan | Add the herbs and wine | Turn up the heat and cook until most of the liquid has evaporated | Add the tomato purée, yeast extract and mustard and stir | Pour in the vegetable stock, bring to the boil, reduce the heat and leave to simmer for 10–12 minutes | Strain the liquid through the sieve into the bowl | Wipe the pan clean | Pour the strained liquid back into the pan and put it back on the heat

Add the water to a mug | Add the flour and whisk with a fork or whisk until there are no lumps | Pour into the pan and whisk to combine | Simmer, whisking all the time, for 5 minutes, until thickened | Taste, season and serve

ULTIMATE NUT ROAST

This is no ordinary nut roast. This is richly flavoured, amazingly moist and will make a wonderful centrepiece at any roast dinner. Use a food processor for chopping the veg to speed up the prep time, or you can even make the whole nut roast the day before – just give it 5–10 more minutes if you're cooking it straight from the fridge.

SERVES 8

100g walnuts
100g pecans
100g hazelnuts
100g cooked chestnuts
2 large parsnips (about 400g)
2 red onions
3 garlic cloves
1 fresh red chilli
1 carrot (about 150g)
100g chestnut mushrooms
8 sprigs fresh thyme
2 sprigs fresh rosemary
1 sprig fresh sage
2 tbsp olive oil
100g wholemeal breadcrumbs
200ml vegetable stock
¼ tsp ground nutmeg
¼ tsp ground allspice
¼ tsp smoked paprika
1 clementine
3 tbsp dried cranberries
sea salt and black pepper
fresh cranberries, to decorate

Preheat oven to 180°C | Grease and line a 450g loaf tin with parchment paper | Baking tray | Medium saucepan of boiling salted water on a high heat | Potato masher | Fine grater or Microplane | Deep-sided frying pan | Food processor | Foil

Spread the walnuts, pecans and hazelnuts over a baking tray | Put the tray in the oven for 8 minutes | Set aside to cool | Crumble the chestnuts

Peel and chop the parsnips into 2cm cubes | Add them to the pan of salted water and cook for 15–18 minutes, until tender | Take off the heat, drain and tip back into the pan | Mash

Prepare the rest of the veg and herbs | Peel and finely chop the red onions | Peel and grate the garlic | Rip the stem from the chilli and slice thinly | Peel and finely grate the carrot | Finely chop the mushrooms | Remove the leaves from the herbs by running your thumb and forefinger from the top to the base of the stems (the leaves should easily come away) | Reserve a few sprigs of thyme for garnish and finely chop the rest

Place the frying pan over a medium heat and add the oil | Add the onions and stir for 15 minutes, until really brown and caramelised, stirring regularly to prevent burning | Add the garlic and chilli and cook for 1 minute | Add the carrot and mushrooms and cook until the mushrooms are sweating and the carrot is softening, about 10 minutes | Add the breadcrumbs, vegetable stock, chopped herbs and spices and fold them into the rest of the ingredients | Take the pan off the heat

Pour half the roasted nuts into the food processor and blitz to a meal | Finely chop the rest of the nuts | Add all the nuts to the pan | Zest the clementine into the pan (you can eat the fruit) | Tip in the mashed parsnips and dried cranberries and fold everything together to form a thick, textured dough | Taste and season

Tip the mixture into the prepared tin and smooth the top with a spatula | Cover with foil | Put the tin in the oven and bake for 80 minutes, removing the foil after 1 hour

Take the tin out of the oven and leave to cool for 30 minutes | Carefully remove the nut roast from the tin, decorate with the reserved thyme sprigs and some fresh cranberries | Sprinkle with sea salt and serve with all the trimmings

BOSH XMAS

Our Christmas table looks just like the one on pages 132–133, and in the middle is our amazing Criss-Cross that will be sure to impress your guests. There's quite a lot to make and prep here, so follow the timings below for a perfect festive feast. The recipes are also great on their own as sides for other meals so don't just save them for the big day!

1 x portion Christmas Criss-Cross
    ingredients (see page 134)
2 x portions Brussels Sprouts with
    Maple Mushrooms (see page 137)
1 x portion Ultimate Roast Stuffing Balls
    (see page 142)
2 x portions Clementine Roasted Root
    Vegetables (see page 138)
1 x portion Perfect Gravy (see page 143)
2 x portions Crisp, Fluffy, Perfect Roast
    Potatoes (see page 141)
2 x portions Bangers in Blankets
    (see page 137)
cranberry sauce, to serve, optional
mint sauce, to serve, optional

Christmas Eve Preheat oven to 180°C | 3 x lined baking trays | Food processor | Deep frying pan | 4 large airtight containers or several smaller ones | 3 roasting tins | 2 large saucepans | Foil | Potato masher or stick blender

First get the mushrooms for your **Christmas Criss-Cross** into the oven | Prep the **Maple Mushrooms** and put them in the oven | Prep the rest of the filling for the **Criss-Cross** | Put the walnuts for the **stuffing** in the oven

Take the walnuts and mushrooms for the **Maple Mushrooms** out of the oven and let them cool | Take out the mushrooms for the **Criss-Cross** and leave to cool | Transfer to separate containers, label them and put them in the fridge | Clean out the food processor

Turn the oven up to 190°C | Prep the beetroot for the **roast vegetables** and put them in the oven on the top shelf | Prep the vegetables for the **Perfect Gravy** and put them on the middle shelf | Prep the carrots for the **roast veg** and put them on the bottom shelf

Meanwhile, continue making your stuffing mixture | Boil your **Brussels**, drain, cool, label and refrigerate | Keep an eye on the veg in the oven and take them out when they're cooked | Nestle the beetroot into the carrots and set them aside to cool, cover with foil and leave overnight (or label and refrigerate) | Lower the oven to 180°C

Roll your **stuffing balls** and bake them | Let them cool, cover in foil and leave in the fridge overnight

Meanwhile, finish making your **gravy** | Turn off the heat, put a lid on the pan and leave overnight

Prep and boil your **potatoes**, steam dry and transfer to a container

Christmas Day Preheat oven to 180°C | Foil | 1 x baking sheet | 3 more baking trays | Frying pan | Pastry brush, optional | At least 12 cocktail sticks | Line 2 plates with kitchen paper

In the morning, take all the food out of the fridge to come up to room temperature

Whack the oven up to 220°C and get your **potatoes** in on the middle shelf

Construct your **Criss-Cross** and put it in the fridge

Prep your **Bangers in Blankets** so that they're ready to go in the oven

Take the **potatoes** out, loosely cover with foil and set aside | Lower the heat to 180°C

Put the **Criss-Cross** on the middle shelf of the oven for 25 minutes | Put the baked almonds for the **Brussels** in for the last 10 minutes

Take out the mushrooms | Take out the almonds, tip them on to a plate and tip the walnuts for the **roasted vegetables** on to the tray | Glaze the **Criss-Cross**, then put it back in | Put the **Bangers in Blankets** on the bottom shelf | Put the walnuts on the top shelf

After 10 minutes, remove the walnuts and put the **roasted veg** in, uncovered | Chop the walnuts | Put the gravy on to heat up

Boil a kettle and pour the water over the **Brussels** to warm them up | Drain and finish cooking the dish

Take the **Criss-Cross** and **roasted veg** out of the oven | Put the **potatoes** back in the oven to warm up | Put the stuffing in the oven to heat through | Add the walnuts and beetroot to the **roasted veg**

Pile your **Brussels** into a serving bowl | Stack your **Bangers in Blankets** and **Stuffing Balls** high on plates | Serve your **roasted vegetables** and **Crisp, Fluffy, Perfect Roast Potatoes** in their tins | Pour your **Perfect Gravy** into a jug | Get everyone seated and bring in your **Christmas Criss-Cross** | Merry Christmas!

Pictured on pages 132–133

CHRISTMAS CRISS-CROSS

SERVES 8

500g chestnut mushrooms
olive oil, for drizzling
8 sprigs fresh thyme
4 sprigs fresh rosemary
2 sprigs fresh sage
8 garlic cloves
4 eschalion (banana) shallots
1 carrot
1 celery stick
4 sun-dried tomatoes, plus 3 tbsp
    oil from the jar
200g cooked chestnuts
200g pecans
200ml red wine
2½ tbsp cranberry sauce
1 bay leaf
½ tsp ground nutmeg
½ tsp ground cinnamon
100g dried breadcrumbs
2 x 320g sheets ready-rolled
    plant-based puff pastry
1 tbsp maple syrup
2 tbsp unsweetened plant-based milk,
    plus extra for brushing
salt and black pepper

Preheat oven to 180°C | Foil | Roasting tin | Fine grater or Microplane | Food processor | Deep-sided frying pan | Baking sheet | Pastry brush, optional

Start by cooking the mushrooms | Lay a sheet of foil over the roasting tin | Sort through the mushrooms and find 10 of the best-looking ones, making sure you're left with about 300g mushrooms | Place the selected mushrooms in the middle of the foil | Drizzle over a little olive oil and sprinkle over a little salt and pepper | Lay half the thyme, rosemary and sage sprigs on top along with 3 of the garlic cloves | Wrap the mushrooms tightly in the foil and put the tin in the oven | Bake for 30 minutes

Meanwhile prep the rest of the veg and herbs | Peel and thinly slice the shallots | Peel and finely grate the carrot | Finely dice the celery | Thinly slice the sun-dried tomatoes | Peel and finely grate the rest of the garlic cloves | Remove the leaves from the remaining thyme and rosemary sprigs by running your thumb and forefinger from the top to the base of the stems (the leaves should easily come away), then finely chop | Pick the leaves from the sage sprig and finely chop

Put the remaining mushrooms in the food processor and blitz to mince | Scrape into a bowl and clean out the food processor | Add half the chestnuts and all of the pecans to the clean food processor and blitz to a meal | Roughly chop the remaining chestnuts

Spoon the sun-dried tomato oil into the frying pan and put the pan over a medium heat | Add the shallots and fry for 5 minutes, until soft | Add the sun-dried tomatoes and garlic and stir for 1 minute | Add the carrots, celery, rosemary, thyme and sage and stir for 4–5 minutes | Add the minced mushrooms to the pan, increase the heat to high and cook for 10 minutes, until the mushrooms are well sweated | Pour over the red wine and cranberry sauce | Add the bay leaf | Simmer for 6–7 minutes, until most of the liquid has evaporated | Reduce the heat, add the ground nutmeg and cinnamon and stir for 1 minute

Take the roasted mushrooms out of the oven, turn off the heat and open the foil | Transfer the mushrooms to a plate and pour the cooking liquid into a mixing bowl | Add the breadcrumbs and nut meal and mix everything together with a spoon | Tip in the mushroom mince, removing the bay leaf | Fold everything together to form a thick, textured dough | Leave to cool to room temperature

Lay one sheet of puff pastry on the baking sheet | Spread half the mushroom mixture lengthways down the middle of the pastry | Use your hands to mould it into a flat rectangular shape, leaving at least 5cm of pastry on each side | Place the roasted mushrooms along the top of the mixture in two neat rows | Layer the rest of the mixture over the top, encasing the mushrooms completely | Smooth and shape into a neat rectangular mound

Brush a little milk around the exposed pastry edge using a pastry brush or your finger | Lay the second pastry sheet over the filling and smooth it down well, ensuring there are no air bubbles | Seal the edges by pressing the pastry sheets together all the way around the filling with your fingers | Trim any excess pastry from the edges, making sure you leave a 1.5cm crust around the base of the Criss-Cross | Use a fork to crimp all around the edges of the pastry to firmly seal the pastry

Take a sharp knife and score a criss-cross pattern across the top of the whole Criss-Cross | Pierce a few air vents in the top of the pastry | If you're feeling creative, cut a few decorative shapes from the excess pastry and place them on top of your Criss-Cross | Place in the fridge for 20 minutes | Preheat the oven to 180°C

Take the Criss-Cross out of the fridge and put it in the hot oven | Bake for 25 minutes

Meanwhile, make a glaze by pouring the maple syrup and milk into a small dish and mixing together | Take the Criss-Cross out of the oven and brush it all over with the glaze | Place back in the oven and bake until golden brown and crispy, about 25 minutes | Remove from the oven

Cut into slices and serve immediately with all the trimmings

BRUSSELS SPROUTS WITH MAPLE MUSHROOMS

SERVES 4

200g mixed mushrooms
4 tbsp olive oil
1 tbsp maple syrup
1 tsp smoked salt
½ tsp smoked paprika
½ tsp black pepper, plus a little extra
    for seasoning
25g flaked almonds
500g Brussels sprouts
2 eschalion (banana) shallots
2 fresh bay leaves
salt

Preheat oven to 180°C | Line 2 baking trays | Large saucepan of boiling salted water on a high heat | Frying pan

Chop the mushrooms into 5mm-thick slices and spread over one of the baking trays | Drizzle over 2 tablespoons of the olive oil and the maple syrup | Sprinkle over the smoked salt, smoked paprika and pepper | Toss well to coat | Put the tray in the oven for 25 minutes, turning halfway

Meanwhile, spread the flaked almonds over the second baking tray | Put the tray in the oven for 10 minutes | Remove and set aside to cool

Meanwhile, trim off any old outer leaves from the sprouts | Put the sprouts in the pan of boiling salted water and cook for 5–6 minutes | Drain and set aside

Peel and thinly slice the shallots | Put the frying pan over a medium heat and add the remaining 2 tablespoons olive oil | When the pan is hot, add the shallots with a pinch of salt and fry for 2–3 minutes, until soft | Add the bay leaves and drained sprouts | Take the mushroom lardons out of the oven and transfer to the frying pan | Cook for 3–4 minutes

Tip the cooked sprouts and mushrooms into a bowl | Sprinkle over the toasted flaked almonds | Season to perfection and serve

BANGERS IN BLANKETS

MAKES 12

6 plant-based sausages
1 medium aubergine

FOR THE MARINADE
4 tbsp olive oil
1½ tbsp maple syrup
½ tsp smoked salt
1½ tsp smoked paprika
½ tsp black pepper

Preheat oven to 190°C | Line a baking tray | Microwavable plate, optional | At least 12 cocktail sticks

If your sausages are frozen, put them on a microwavable plate and cook on full for 90 seconds to defrost | Alternatively, defrost in the fridge overnight

Pour all the ingredients for the marinade into a bowl | Mix with a fork until the salt has dissolved

Peel and trim the aubergine, then cut it lengthways into quarters | Cut each quarter into thin slices, roughly 3mm thick (you will need 12 thin slices) | Save any leftovers for a different recipe, like our Big Breakfast Bagel on page 258 | Toss in the smoky oil and marinate for 5 minutes

Cut all the sausages in half across the middle | Trim the cut edges to match the round ends | Tightly wrap the sausages in the marinated aubergine slices, securing them with cocktail sticks | Lay them on the lined baking tray | Put the tray in the oven and bake for 10 minutes | Baste the sausages with the juices in the pan and cook for another 5 minutes | Baste again and cook for another 10 minutes | Baste once more and cook for another 5 minutes | Turn up the heat and give them a final blast for 5 minutes | Take out of the oven and serve immediately

CLEMENTINE ROASTED ROOT VEGETABLES

SERVES 4 *as a side*

500g heritage carrots
4 medium beetroot
2 tbsp olive oil
2 tbsp water
1 tsp sea salt, plus a little extra
    for seasoning
2 clementines
2 tbsp balsamic vinegar
1 tbsp pomegranate molasses
10g fresh thyme
1 bay leaf
100g walnuts
black pepper

Preheat oven to 190°C | **Foil** | **2 baking trays** | **Roasting tin**

Trim the carrots, peel them if the skins are tough and cut any large ones in half lengthways

Trim the beetroot, peel if desired and cut them in half

Lay a large sheet of foil on a baking tray | Place the beetroot in the middle and drizzle over 1 tablespoon of the olive oil, the water and a little salt and pepper | Turn the beetroot to coat | Scrunch up the foil to make a package, making sure there are no gaps to let out any steam | Put the tray in the oven to steam for 1 hour

Meanwhile, put the carrots in the roasting tin | Zest one of the clementines over the carrots, then cut it in half horizontally and squeeze over the juice, catching any pips in your other hand | Pour over the balsamic vinegar, pomegranate molasses and the rest of the olive oil | Season with salt and pepper and stir to coat the carrots | Cut the remaining clementine in half horizontally and put it in the tin along with the thyme and bay leaf

When the beetroot has been in the oven for 30 minutes, put the carrots in and roast them for 25 minutes | Check if they are cooked and if they're still hard return the tin to the oven for up to 10 minutes more

Put the walnuts on the second baking tray | 10 minutes before the beetroot are ready to come out of the oven, put the walnuts in and bake, checking after 8 minutes to make sure they're not burning | Take the tray out of the oven, transfer the nuts to a chopping board, leave to cool slightly and then roughly chop

Take the beetroot out of the oven and put the tray on a heatproof surface | Open the foil, leave to cool a little then cut the beetroot into wedges

Remove the roasting tin from the oven | Tip in the beetroot wedges and toasted walnuts and stir them around in the caramelised carrot juices | Decorate with the roasted clementine and serve immediately

CRISPY, FLUFFY, PERFECT ROAST POTATOES

1.5kg Maris Piper or other floury
  potatoes
3 tbsp salt
4 tbsp olive oil
1 garlic bulb
2 sprigs fresh sage
10 sprigs fresh thyme
4 sprigs fresh rosemary

Preheat oven to 220°C | Half fill a large bowl with cold water | Large saucepan | Large baking tray | Line 2 plates with kitchen paper

Peel the potatoes and place them in the bowl of cold water to get rid of the excess starch | Drain and tip into the saucepan | Cover with cold water | Add half the salt | Put the pan on a high heat and bring to the boil | Boil for 8 minutes | Tip the potatoes into a colander and leave to steam dry for 5 minutes

Shake the potatoes in the colander to rough the edges (this will give you a perfect, crunchy crust) | Spread the potatoes over the baking tray so that they're not touching | Pour over the olive oil and sprinkle over the remaining salt | Turn the potatoes to make sure they're well coated

Put the tray in the oven and roast the potatoes for 30 minutes | Break the garlic bulb into separate cloves | Remove the potatoes from the oven and add the garlic, sage, thyme and rosemary sprigs | Turn the potatoes again to coat | Put the tray back in the oven and roast for a further 40–50 minutes, until the skins are incredibly crispy and a deep golden colour

Take the tray out of the oven | Transfer the potatoes to the plates covered with kitchen paper to drain the excess oil | Serve with a full roast and all the trimmings!

ULTIMATE ROAST STUFFING BALLS

MAKES 16

25g walnuts
1 small onion
1 parsnip (about 150g)
1 ripe Conference pear
200g wholemeal bread
10g fresh sage
1 tbsp olive oil, plus extra for greasing
25g dried cranberries
⅛ tsp ground allspice
⅛ tsp ground nutmeg
125ml unsweetened plant-based milk

Preheat oven to 180°C | Line a baking tray | Food processor | Medium saucepan

....

Spread the walnuts over the baking tray | Put the tray in the oven for 8–9 minutes, until the nuts are lightly toasted | Remove, transfer to a chopping board and roughly chop

Peel and finely dice the onion, parsnip and pear | Remove and discard the crusts from the bread then blitz the bread to make breadcrumbs | Roughly chop the sage

Place the saucepan over a medium heat and add the oil | Add the onion and fry for 5–6 minutes, stirring, until soft and translucent | Add the parsnip and pears, stir and cook for 6–7 minutes | Add half the breadcrumbs to the pan and stir for 3–4 minutes until they start to turn golden | Take the pan off the heat and tip the contents into a large bowl

Add the sage, walnuts, dried cranberries, allspice, nutmeg, plant-based milk and remaining breadcrumbs to the bowl and mix well to bring the ingredients together

Lightly oil the lined baking tray you used before | Use your hands to roll 16 walnut-sized balls of stuffing and place them on the tray | Put them in the oven and bake for 35–40 minutes until golden and firm to the touch | Remove from the oven and serve

PERFECT GRAVY

MAKES ABOUT 800ml

1 large onion
2 carrots (about 350g)
1 leek
2 celery sticks
4 garlic cloves
1 bay leaf
a small bunch of fresh thyme
1 sprig fresh rosemary
3 tbsp olive oil
2 tsp salt
1 tsp black pepper
50g dried porcini mushrooms
2½ tbsp flour
4 tbsp water
500ml vegetable stock
1 tbsp soy sauce
100ml port

Preheat oven to 190°C | **Large roasting tin** | **Kettle boiled** | **Potato masher or stick blender** | **2 large saucepans**

....

First roast the vegetables | Peel and quarter the onion | Trim the carrots, leek and celery and cut them into 4–5cm pieces | Put all the vegetables into the roasting tin along with the unpeeled garlic cloves, bay leaf, thyme and rosemary | Drizzle with the olive oil and sprinkle over the salt and pepper | Place in the oven and roast for 45 minutes, tossing once halfway through

Put the porcini mushrooms into a mug and fill it with hot water | Leave to soak while the vegetables roast

Take the vegetables out of the oven | Peel the skins off the garlic cloves then mash all the vegetables in the tin with a potato masher or pulse with a stick blender until mushy but not smooth | Transfer to one of the large saucepans

Put the flour into a mug and add the water | Whisk with a fork until all the lumps have dissolved | Add to the saucepan | Pour in the porcini mushrooms and soaking liquid | Add the vegetable stock, soy sauce and port | Place on a high heat | Stir continuously until the gravy is bubbling then reduce the heat and simmer for about 30 minutes, checking regularly to ensure it doesn't stick to the pan

When the gravy reaches your ideal thickness, pour it through a sieve into the second pan, forcing the gravy through with a wooden spoon | Put the pan over a very low heat to keep warm until you are ready to serve, then transfer to a serving jug or gravy boat

It'll be no surprise to you that we enjoy a cocktail from time to time, but making them yourself at home does involve a fair bit of work. A cocktail jug is a much more efficient way to enjoy a tasty drink with friends! With the exception of the mango lassi, all of these drinks lend themselves really well to different fruity flavours so try varying the fruit or berries in the agua fresca, sangria or dacquiri for a whole lot more cocktail fun.

STRAWBERRY DAIQUIRI SLUSHY

SERVES 4

Liquidiser | **1-litre jug**

450g strawberries, frozen if possible
4 limes
6 tbsp agave syrup
250ml white rum
20g fresh mint
ice

Hull the strawberries, if fresh, spread over a baking tray and put in the freezer for at least 2 hours or ideally overnight

Cut all the limes in half and squeeze the juice into the liquidiser | Add the syrup, frozen strawberries and rum and blend until liquid | Fill the liquidiser to the top with ice and pulse until you've reach a slushy consistency | Pour the daiquiri into a jug, add the mint and serve immediately

NAUGHTY AGUA FRESCA

SERVES 4

Liquidiser | **1-litre jug**

600g strawberries
1 small pineapple (about 1.3kg
    unpeeled weight)
1 tbsp caster sugar
100ml vodka
100ml cold water
ice

Hull the strawberries | Peel and core the pineapple and chop it into chunks | Put the fruit, caster sugar, vodka and water into the liquidiser and blend until liquid | Fill a quarter of the jug with ice and pour over the agua fresca | Serve immediately

CHEEKY MANGO LASSI

4 ripe mangoes
500g dairy-free yoghurt
2—4 tbsp agave syrup
2 limes
100ml white rum
ice

Liquidiser | 1-litre jug

Slice the mangoes lengthways down either side of the stone | Spoon the flesh into the liquidiser and blend to a purée | Add the dairy-free yoghurt and agave syrup | Zest both the limes into the liquidiser, then cut them in half and squeeze in the juice | Add the rum | Blend until completely smooth | Fill a quarter of the jug with ice and pour over the lassi | Serve immediately

FRUITY SANGRIA

200g strawberries
1 orange
2 ripe peaches
3 tbsp brown sugar
700ml Spanish red wine
200ml orange juice
50ml brandy
a little sparkling water, optional
a small bunch of mint
ice

1-litre jug

Hull the strawberries and cut them in half | Cut the orange into slices | Cut the peaches in half, cut out the stones and slice | Put all the fruit into the jug | Sprinkle over the brown sugar | Pour in the red wine, orange juice and brandy | Taste and add a little sparkling water or extra brandy if you like | Put the bunch of mint in the jug and fill it to the top with ice | Stir everything together with a long wooden spoon and serve immediately

Pictured on pages 146—147

STRAWBERRY
DAIQUIRI SLUSHY

NAUGHTY AGUA
FRESCA

CHEEKY MANGO
LASSI

FRUITY SANGRIA

SIDES & SHARERS

Henry's favourite
Party Poppers with BOSH! BBQ Sauce

Ian's favourite
Wild West Wings

CAMEMBOSH HEDGEHOG

This always generates big smiles in all who behold it! Big thanks to Ellie from Kinda Co (makers of incredible plant-based cheeses) for the original recipe, which we collaborated on together in the early days of BOSH! Tapioca flour is crucial for optimum gooeyness, so do seek some out. To get ahead, make the cheese the day before and keep it in the fridge.

SERVES 6

75g cashews
1 x 400g fresh tiger loaf
2 garlic cloves
1 tbsp tapioca flour
1½ tsp salt, plus extra for seasoning
3 tsp nutritional yeast
1 tsp apple cider vinegar
150ml warm water
1 sprig fresh rosemary
1 tsp olive oil
black pepper

FOR THE HERB OIL
2 garlic cloves
1 sprig fresh rosemary
1 tsp salt
¼ tsp black pepper
8 tbsp olive oil

Preheat oven to 180°C | Line a baking sheet | Line a 12cm ovenproof dish with parchment paper | Small saucepan of boiling water on a medium heat | Pestle and mortar, optional | Liquidiser | Kettle boiled

First make the cheese | Add the cashews to the pan of hot water and boil for 20 minutes to soften | Remove from the heat, drain and leave to cool

Prepare the loaf | Use a bread knife to cut even slices across the top of the loaf, 3cm apart, making sure you don't cut all the way through as the base needs to remain intact | Turn the loaf 90 degrees and cut across the first slices to make a criss-cross pattern

To make the herb oil, peel and roughly chop the garlic | Remove the leaves from the rosemary by running your thumb and forefinger from the top to the base of the stem (the leaves should easily come away) and finely chop | Put the garlic, rosemary, salt and pepper into the mortar and bash them with the pestle to make a paste (or put the ingredients in a small bowl and use the end of a rolling pin) | Pour the olive oil into the mortar and mix with a fork

Put the loaf on the baking sheet | Use a pastry brush or teaspoon to drizzle the herb oil deep inside the cuts | Put the baking sheet in the oven and cook for 25–30 minutes, until golden and toasted

Meanwhile, finish the cheese | Peel 1 of the garlic cloves and put it in the liquidiser | Add the drained cashews, tapioca flour, salt, nutritional yeast, apple cider vinegar and warm water | Blend to a smooth cream

Pour the cashew cream into the saucepan, taste and season with salt and pepper | Put the saucepan on a medium heat and cook, stirring constantly, for 2 minutes, until slightly thickened | Pour into the parchment-lined dish

Peel the remaining garlic clove and cut it into sticks | Remove the rosemary needles | Gently push the garlic sticks and rosemary needles into the top of the cashew cheese so that they stick out the top | Drizzle over the olive oil and sprinkle over a little black pepper

When ready to serve, put the cashew cheese in the oven alongside the bread and bake for the final 12–15 minutes, until the cheese has formed a skin and the colour has darkened | Remove and serve immediately

SUSHI CUPCAKES

This is a fun take on sushi! This fantastic technique allows you to exercise your creativity and create food that's tasty, healthy and truly Instagram-worthy. Tag us in your photos with #sushicupcakes. We put hoisin sauce in the middle of our cupcakes, but you can add whatever you like. Wasabi and ginger is a great traditional filling.

MAKES 12

400g sushi rice
30ml rice vinegar
25g caster sugar
½ tsp salt
12 nori sheets
6 tsp hoisin sauce
black sesame seeds, for sprinkling
pickled ginger, to serve
soy sauce, to serve
wasabi, to serve, optional

FOR THE VEGETABLE TOPPINGS
1 red pepper
1 carrot
¼ cucumber
1 small avocado
10 fresh chives
5 radishes

FOR THE DIPPING SAUCE
sriracha
egg-free mayonnaise

Small saucepan | Grease a baking tray with flavourless oil (such as vegetable or sunflower) | 14cm saucer | Ruler, optional | 12-hole (or 2 x 6-hole) muffin tin

Cook the sushi rice following the instructions on the packet, ensuring that it is dry and sticky when cooked

Put the saucepan on a medium heat | Pour in the rice vinegar, sugar and salt and heat until the sugar has dissolved | Let cool to room temperature, then pour over the cooked rice, gently stirring until all the liquid is absorbed | Spread the rice over the greased baking tray and let cool to room temperature, when it should be dry but sticky

Stack the nori sheets and lay the saucer on top | Cut around it to make nori circles | Find the centre of the nori stack and cut a neat, straight slit from the centre to the outer edges | Take one circle and fashion a cone that is roughly 8cm wide at the base | Wet your finger and lightly brush along the slit to stick it in place | Put the cone in one of the muffin holes | Repeat to fill all the muffin holes

Wet your hands and roll a golf ball-sized ball of rice | Poke a hole in the centre and pour in ½ teaspoon hoisin sauce | Pack more rice over the hole to seal in the sauce | Smooth the outside and place in one of the nori muffin cases | Repeat to fill all the cases

Get all your toppings ready | Cut the pepper in half, cut out the stems and seeds and thinly slice | Peel the carrot and cut into matchsticks, thin rounds or ribbons | Cut the cucumber in the same way | Halve and carefully stone the avocado by tapping the stone firmly with the heel of a knife so that it lodges in the stone, then twist and remove, then finely slice | Chop the chives | Trim and thinly slice the radishes

Make a quick dipping sauce by stirring sriracha into the egg-free mayonnaise to taste | Finely chop the pickled ginger

Decorate your sushi cupcakes with the prepared vegetables and sprinkle them with black sesame seeds | Serve with soy sauce, wasabi, if using, pickled ginger and the dipping sauce on the side

LOADED POTATO NACHOS

This dish is perfect movie night fodder. Try it with sweet potatoes too – just keep an eye on them to get the right crispiness. The sour cream and salsa will keep in the fridge for up to 3 days, but the guac should be eaten the day you make it – it keeps in the fridge for a few hours if you squeeze a good amount of lemon juice over the top and cover the bowl.

SERVES 4

6 tbsp olive oil
1½ tbsp garlic powder
1½ tbsp onion powder
1 tbsp paprika
2 tsp cayenne pepper
2 tsp salt
1 tsp black pepper
700g Maris Piper potatoes
200g cherry tomatoes
100g dairy-free pizza cheese
100g pickled jalapeños
1 x 400g tin refried beans

FOR THE TOPPINGS
Sour Cream (shop-bought or see opposite)
Salsa (shop-bought or see opposite)
Green Chilli Guacamole (shop-bought or see opposite)
10g fresh coriander leaves, optional

Preheat oven to 180°C | Grater | Liquidiser | Large mixing bowl | Line 3 baking sheets | Lasagne dish | Foil

First cover the potatoes in a spicy coating | Put the olive oil, garlic powder, onion powder, paprika, cayenne pepper, salt and pepper into a bowl and mix with a fork | Cut the potatoes into 2.5mm-thick slices and add them to the bowl | Toss to coat evenly in the flavoured oil

Spread the potato slices over the baking sheets | Put the sheets in the oven and bake for 20 minutes, until golden brown, swapping the sheets between the shelves halfway through to ensure even cooking | Remove from the oven and set aside to cool to room temperature

While the potatoes are cooking and cooling, get your fillings and toppings ready | Finely chop the cherry tomatoes | Grate the dairy-free cheese | Finely chop the jalapeños | Make the sour cream, salsa and guacamole (see opposite)

Now layer up the nachos | Cover the bottom of the lasagne dish with potato slices | Spread over some refried beans, cherry tomatoes, jalapeños and dairy-free cheese | Repeat to layer up the dish, finishing with a layer of nachos and light sprinkling of cheese | Cover with foil, then pierce it a few times with a fork | Put the dish in the oven and bake for 20 minutes, removing the foil halfway through, until the nachos around the edges of the dish are crisping up

When the nachos are cooked, drizzle over the sour cream | Spoon over the salsa | Dollop over the guacamole | Sprinkle over the coriander leaves, if using, and serve immediately

Pictured on pages 156–157

SOUR CREAM

SERVES 4

Liquidiser

½ lemon
200g cashews
2 tsp nutritional yeast
½ tsp salt
125ml water

Squeeze the lemon juice into the liquidiser, catching any pips in your other hand | Add all the rest of the ingredients | Blend to a very smooth cream | Taste, season with more salt and loosen with a little water if necessary to reach your desired consistency and serve or refrigerate until needed

QUICK SALSA

SERVES 4

Fine grater or Microplane

4 large tomatoes
4 spring onions
10g fresh coriander
10g pickled jalapeños
1 lime
1 small garlic clove
¾ tsp salt

Finely chop the tomatoes | Thinly slice the spring onions | Pick the leaves from the coriander and chop roughly | Chop the pickled jalapeños | Cut the lime in half | Peel and grate the garlic

Squeeze the lime juice into a bowl | Add all the rest of the salsa ingredients and mix together | Pour into a sieve and leave to drain for 2–3 minutes | Tip the salsa back into the bowl and serve, or cover and refrigerate until needed

GREEN CHILLI GUACAMOLE

SERVES 4

Fine grater or Microplane

3 ripe avocados
4 cherry tomatoes
½ small red onion
1 small garlic clove
1 fresh green chilli
1 lime
½ lemon
½ tsp salt

Halve and carefully stone the avocados by tapping the stone firmly with the heel of a knife so that it lodges in the stone, then twist and remove | Scoop out the flesh | Finely chop the tomatoes | Peel and mince the red onion | Peel and finely grate the garlic | Rip the stem from the chilli and chop finely | Put all the prepared ingredients into a large bowl | Cut the lime in half and squeeze in the juice | Squeeze in the lemon juice, catching any pips with your other hand | Mash well with a fork until really creamy | Taste, season with salt and serve or cover and refrigerate until needed

SATAY SUMMER ROLLS

There's something so satisfying about making your own summer rolls. It's a little fiddly but once you've done a couple you'll be in the swing of things. The satay sauce goes really well with Thai crackers or on the side of any Thai meal, so make a batch and keep it in the fridge for up to 2 days. The rolls make an excellent packed lunch too. You'll be the envy of your friends!

MAKES 16

100g dried rice vermicelli
1 large carrot
½ cucumber
100g red cabbage
a small bunch of fresh mint
a small bunch of fresh coriander
a small bunch of fresh Thai basil
a small handful of fresh chives
a small handful of salted roasted peanuts
16 rice paper wrappers

FOR THE CRISPY TOFU
1 x 280g block extra-firm tofu
3 tbsp cornflour
3 tbsp sesame oil

FOR THE DRESSING
1 lime
1 fresh red chilli
2cm piece fresh ginger
1 tsp caster sugar
1 tsp soy sauce
½ tbsp rice vinegar

FOR THE SATAY DIPPING SAUCE
2 limes
1 bird's-eye chilli
1 garlic clove
6 tbsp crunchy peanut butter
2 tbsp soft brown sugar
1 tbsp soy sauce

Tofu press or 2 clean tea towels and a weight such as a heavy book | Medium saucepan | Frying pan | Line a plate with kitchen paper | Fine grater or Microplane

Press the tofu using a tofu press or place it between two clean tea towels, lay it on a plate and put a weight on top | Leave for at least 30 minutes to drain and firm up before you start cooking

Cook the vermicelli following the instructions on the packet | Rinse, drain thoroughly, then tip into a bowl

Cut the tofu into 16 strips about 5mm wide | Put the cornflour into a dish | Add the tofu strips and toss to coat | Place the frying pan over a high heat | Pour in the oil and let it get very hot | Add the tofu strips in batches and fry until crisp and golden | Transfer to kitchen paper to drain

To make the dressing, zest the lime into a bowl, cut it in half and squeeze in the juice | Rip the stem from the chilli and finely chop | Peel the ginger by scraping off the skin with a spoon and grate it into the bowl | Add the sugar, soy sauce and rice vinegar and mix

Prepare the rest of the fresh filling ingredients | Peel the carrot | Cut the carrot and cucumber into matchsticks | Trim and thinly slice the red cabbage | Put the veggies into a bowl and drizzle with 1 tablespoon of the dressing | Drizzle 1 tablespoon of dressing over the noodles

Pick the leaves from the herbs | Snip the chives into 10cm lengths | Roughly chop the roasted peanuts

Now start making your summer rolls | Half fill a bowl with cold water | Submerge a rice wrapper until it is soft and pliable but not completely soggy | Lay on a chopping board | Arrange some herbs, sliced vegetables, a tofu strip, noodles and chopped peanuts down the middle | Bring the bottom edge of the wrapper up over the filling, fold one side over and roll up tightly, then fold down the top to seal | Place on a plate, join-side down | Repeat to use up all the tofu strips

To make the satay dipping sauce, halve the limes and squeeze the juice into a bowl | Rip the stem from the chilli and thinly slice | Peel and grate the garlic | Add all the ingredients to the bowl and mix well

Serve the fresh summer rolls with the dipping sauce on the side

WILD WEST WINGS

These wings are simply incredible. After a trip to L.A. we created this recipe inspired by a Gordon Ramsay video. Our talented foodie friend Clare Gray suggested we try oyster mushrooms instead of seitan, and our Wild West Wings were born! You can also try other mushrooms, such as shiitake. Our chilli sauces are spectacular and keep in a jar in the fridge for up to 2 weeks.

SERVES 4

200ml unsweetened plant-based milk
100g coconut yoghurt (the thicker the better)
1 tsp salt
1–2 lemons
500g oyster mushrooms
175g plain flour
½ tsp black pepper
2 tsp cayenne pepper
1 tsp smoked paprika
1 tsp garlic powder
fresh chives, to garnish
1 fresh red chilli, to garnish
vegetable oil, for frying

Whisk | 2 large mixing bowls | Large saucepan | Cooking thermometer, optional | Kitchen paper

First make the marinade for the mushrooms | Put the milk, coconut yoghurt and salt in a large mixing bowl | Slice the lemons and squeeze in the juice reasonably sparingly, catching any pips in your other hand | The batter shouldn't be too thin | Whisk until there are no lumps | Add the mushrooms and stir to coat | Leave for 10 minutes to marinate

To make a dry coating, put the flour, pepper, cayenne pepper, smoked paprika and garlic powder in the second mixing bowl and mix together with a fork

If you're making your own chilli sauce (see opposite), make it now and set it to one side

Pour oil into the saucepan to a depth of 8cm and heat to 180°C, or until a wooden spoon dipped into the oil sizzles around the edges | Pick the mushrooms out of the marinade and transfer them to the bowl of dry ingredients | Toss until really well coated

Place the mushrooms in the pan, in batches, making sure not to overcrowd the pan | Cook for 4–5 minutes, turning regularly, until deep golden brown | Transfer to the kitchen paper with a slotted spoon for 2 minutes to soak up the excess oil

Place the wings on a serving platter | Drizzle over some chilli sauce and serve the rest in a bowl for dipping | Finely chop the chives and sprinkle over | Rip the stem from the chilli, cut it in half lengthways and remove the seeds if you prefer, then finely chop and scatter over the Wild West Wings

Pictured on pages 158–159

DE LA SEOUL CHILLI SAUCE

MAKES ABOUT 150ml

Fine grater or Microplane | Small pan

....

2 large garlic cloves
2cm piece fresh ginger
1 tbsp sesame oil
3 tbsp maple syrup
1 tbsp soy sauce
3 tbsp sriracha

Peel and grate the garlic | Peel the ginger by scraping off the skin with a spoon and grate | Put the small pan on a medium heat and pour in the sesame oil | Add the garlic and ginger and cook for 3 minutes, until starting to soften | Pour into a dish and add the maple syrup, soy sauce and sriracha | Stir everything together well

WILD WEST CHILLI SAUCE

MAKES ABOUT 150ml

Liquidiser

....

5 mixed chillies (we used fresh red
   chillies, 1 Thai chilli and 1 scotch
   bonnet)
1 red pepper
3 garlic cloves
1 lime
2 roasted red peppers in oil (from a jar)
40g caster sugar
1 tbsp cornflour or plain flour
½ tsp salt
50ml white wine vinegar

Rip the stems from the chillies, cut them in half lengthways and remove the seeds if you prefer a milder sauce | Cut the pepper in half and cut out the stem and seeds, then roughly chop | Peel the garlic cloves | Cut the lime in half and squeeze the juice into the liquidiser | Add all the remaining ingredients and blend to a smooth paste

WILD WEST
CHILLI SAUCE

DE LA SEOUL
CHILLI SAUCE

PARTY POPPERS WITH BOSH! BBQ SAUCE

These popcorn bites are fried twice for incredible crispiness. It's quite a long recipe, so double it and freeze half the poppers after their first fry for up to a month. You can make this quicker by frying just once at 180°C and skipping the extra steps. But those extra steps are definitely worth it!

FOR THE PARTY POPPERS

90g vital wheat gluten
10g nutritional yeast
½ tsp onion powder
½ tsp garlic powder
¼ tsp ground sage
¼ tsp ground thyme
½ tsp sea salt, plus extra for sprinkling
½ tsp black pepper
½ tsp ground cumin
130ml vegetable stock
1½ tbsp olive oil
½ tsp apple cider vinegar
10–15g fresh coriander leaves
½ tbsp chilli flakes
4 tbsp BBQ sauce, shop-bought or use our recipe on page 166, or shop-bought teriyaki sauce, to serve
vegetable oil, for deep-frying

FOR THE BUTTERMILK MARINADE

2 lemons
400ml unsweetened soy milk
200g coconut yoghurt (the thicker the better)
2 tsp salt

FOR THE DRY COATING

300g plain flour, plus extra for dusting
2 tsp cayenne pepper
2 tsp smoked paprika
2 tsp garlic powder
1 tsp black pepper

Clean work surface dusted liberally with flour | Large saucepan with a lid | Kettle boiled | Steamer basket or colander | Large deep-sided frying pan | Cooking thermometer | Line a large plate with kitchen paper | Clear some space in the freezer | Freezer bags

First make the dough for the poppers | Place the vital wheat gluten, nutritional yeast and all the herbs and spices in a large bowl and mix to combine | In a separate bowl or jug mix together the vegetable stock, olive oil and apple cider vinegar | Pour the wet ingredients into the dry ingredients and mix thoroughly until it comes together as a dough

Tip the dough on to the floured work surface and knead for 10 minutes, until the dough becomes uniform and a bit spongy, being careful not to overwork it as it can get tough | Cut into 1cm cubes

Put the large saucepan over a medium-high heat | Pour boiling water into the saucepan until it's 2cm deep | Place the steamer basket or colander on top of the pan and add the seitan cubes | Cover with the lid and simmer for 45 minutes to steam the dough | Check the water every now and then and top it up with boiling water if necessary to stop the pan burning dry | Remove after 45 minutes and set aside to cool to room temperature

To make the buttermilk marinade, cut the lemons in half and squeeze the juice into a bowl, catching any pips in your other hand | Pour in the soy milk, coconut yoghurt and salt | Whisk together well

Now make the dry coating by combining all the ingredients in a separate bowl

Put the cooled dough cubes into the buttermilk marinade and stir to cover | Leave for 10 minutes to marinate

Dip the marinated dough pieces into the dry batter, rolling them around to coat | Now double-dip them in the marinade and roll them in the dry batter for a second time

Continued over the page

For the first fry, pour vegetable oil for deep-frying into the large frying pan so that it comes no more than halfway up the sides | Heat the oil to 130°C (this is a fairly low temperature for deep frying so if you don't have a thermometer, drop a cube of bread into the pan to test the temperature: when it's ready it should float but take a little while to brown) | Transfer some of the battered poppers to the pan using a slotted spoon – do this in batches so the oil stays at the correct temperature | Fry, turning regularly, until light golden brown and a light crust has started to form, about 3 minutes | Transfer to the plate lined with kitchen paper to drain and cool to room temperature, then transfer to freezer bags and put them in the freezer for at least an hour | Keep the oil in the pan to use again later

Once the bites are frozen, take them out of the freezer | Reheat the oil to 180°C, or until a wooden spoon dipped into the oil sizzles around the edges | Fry in batches, for about 5 minutes, until dark golden brown | Transfer to kitchen paper and sprinkle with sea salt

Finely chop the fresh coriander leaves and sprinkle over the poppers along with the chilli flakes | Serve with BBQ sauce or your favourite dip on the side

BOSH! BBQ SAUCE

MAKES ABOUT 250g

1 tbsp vegetable oil
2 small onions
2 fresh red chillies
4cm piece fresh ginger
4 garlic cloves
300ml apple juice
200ml red wine vinegar
150ml soy sauce
4 tbsp tomato ketchup
2 tbsp Dijon mustard
200g light brown sugar

Medium saucepan on a medium heat | Sterilised bottle or jar (see page 39)

Add the oil to the pan | Peel and finely chop the onions and add them to the pan | Cook for 5 minutes, stirring

Rip the stems from the chillies, cut them in half lengthways and remove the seeds if you prefer a milder sauce, then finely chop | Peel the ginger by scraping off the skin with a spoon and finely chop | Peel and finely chop the garlic

Add all of the ingredients to the pan and stir until the sugar dissolves | Bring to the boil then reduce the heat to a low simmer | Cook for 40–45 minutes, until the sauce is thick and you have about 250g | Taste and season | Use it just as it is or for a more typical, smooth sauce, blend in a liquidiser until smooth | Transfer to a sterilised bottle or jar and store in the fridge

BIG BAD BHAJIS WITH SPICY TOMATO CHUTNEY

The ubiquitous Indian snack, the bhaji, gets the BOSH! treatment with the addition of fenugreek seeds and a winner of a chutney. Bhajis are a great way of using up leftover veg – try adding finely match-sticked aubergine, potato, spring onions or Tenderstem broccoli to the mix. Taste the batter as you go and adjust to your preferences.

MAKES 8

2 large white onions
1 garlic clove
5cm piece fresh ginger
1 fresh red chilli
20g fresh coriander
300g gram flour
100g sweetcorn
1 tbsp nigella seeds
1 tbsp ground coriander
1 tbsp ground cumin
1 tbsp salt
1 tbsp garam masala
1 tsp ground fenugreek, optional
1 tsp ground turmeric
200ml water
vegetable oil, for deep-frying

FOR THE SPICY TOMATO CHUTNEY
2 tbsp vegetable oil
½ tsp fenugreek seeds, optional
1 tsp nigella seeds
1 tsp cumin seeds
1 tsp black mustard seeds
1 tsp fennel seeds
5cm piece fresh ginger
1 x 400g tin chopped tomatoes
80g caster sugar
1 tsp salt
1 tbsp chilli flakes

Large saucepan on a medium heat | **Line a large plate with kitchen paper** | **Fine grater or Microplane**

First make the chutney | Pour the oil into the pan and let it heat up | Add the fenugreek seeds, if using | Add the nigella, cumin, black mustard and fennel seeds and fry until the seeds are aromatic and starting to crackle | Peel the ginger by scraping off the skin with a spoon, then grate it into the pan | Stir for 1 minute | Pour in the chopped tomatoes and heat for 2–3 minutes until simmering | Add the sugar and salt and stir until the sugar dissolves | Turn down the heat and let everything simmer gently, stirring occasionally, for 10–12 minutes, until thick and syrupy | Stir in the chilli flakes | Pour the chutney into a heatproof serving dish and leave to cool to room temperature | Clean out the pan

To make the bhajis, peel and thinly slice the onions | Peel and grate the garlic | Peel the ginger by scraping off the skin with a spoon, then finely grate it | Rip the stem from the chilli, cut it in half lengthways and remove the seeds if you prefer a milder flavour, then thinly slice | Rip the leaves from the coriander and dispose of the stems | Put all the bhaji ingredients except for the oil into a bowl | Mix everything together to form a thick, textured batter

Put the clean saucepan back on a medium heat | Pour in the vegetable oil until it's 10–12cm deep | Heat until a wooden spoon dipped into the oil sizzles around the edges

Roll a golf-ball-sized piece of batter in your hands | Carefully squash the ball so that it's about 2cm thick | Repeat to use up all the bhaji batter | Carefully place a few bhajis in the oil and fry for 3–4 minutes, until golden and crispy | Transfer to the plate lined with kitchen paper using a slotted spoon | Repeat to cook all the bhajis | Serve immediately with the spicy tomato chutney

BBQ BEANS WITH MUSHROOM BURNT ENDS

We love this recipe. Home-made baked beans are so easy yet feel like such a treat! The burnt ends give the whole dish a wonderfully smoky flavour. We also suggest pairing this with our Baking Tray Breakfast (see page 270) for the ultimate cooked breakfast.

(see page 270)

SERVES 1–2

½ onion
2 garlic cloves
1 tbsp olive oil
1 tbsp tomato purée
¼ tsp smoked paprika
¼ tsp chilli powder
¼ tsp dried thyme
1 tbsp light brown sugar
1 tbsp light soy sauce
1 x 400g tin cannellini beans
200g passata
salt and black pepper

FOR THE MUSHROOM BURNT ENDS
200g mixed mushrooms
1 tbsp olive oil
3 tbsp good-quality BBQ sauce
salt

Large frying pan | Medium saucepan

First make the burnt ends | Thinly slice the mushrooms | Add the tablespoon of olive oil to the frying pan and place over a medium-high heat | Add the mushrooms | Sprinkle over a good pinch of salt | Fry, stirring regularly, until very browned but not burnt, about 10 minutes | Add the BBQ sauce to the pan and stir to coat | Cook for another 1–3 minutes, until the sauce has fully coated and caramelised around the mushrooms and the mushrooms have blackened (but are not burnt)

Meanwhile, make the BBQ beans | Peel and finely chop the onion and garlic | Add the tablespoon of olive oil to the saucepan and place over a medium heat | Add the onion and sauté for 5 minutes | Add the garlic and sauté for 3 minutes | Add the tomato purée, smoked paprika, chilli powder, thyme, sugar and soy sauce and stir them into the onions | Cook for a further 2 minutes

Drain and rinse the cannellini beans, then add them to the pan and stir | Cook for another 2–3 minutes | Pour over the passata and let it simmer until the sauce has thickened, about 5 minutes | Taste and season

Serve up the beans and spoon the mushroom burnt ends on top, stirring some through the beans

NOTTING HILL PATTIES

These patties are perfect for a summer party, whether it's a BBQ or a West London carnival! They go great with Encona dipping sauce or with our sauce on page 166. This recipe makes enough for six awesome little patties, and one or two should easily be enough for a delicious lunch on the go, so wrap 'em up in foil and take them with you!

They go great with Encona dipping sauce or with our sauce on page 166.

MAKES 6

110g dairy-free butter
225g plain flour, plus extra for dusting
1 tsp ground turmeric
¼ tsp salt
2–3 tbsp water
unsweetened plant-based milk,
    for brushing

FOR THE FILLING
6 plant-based sausages
2 garlic cloves
3cm piece fresh ginger
5 spring onions
4 medium tomatoes
2 sprigs fresh thyme
2 tbsp olive oil
1 tbsp soy sauce
¼ tsp ground allspice
½ tsp black pepper
2 tsp Encona West Indian hot sauce,
    plus a little extra
1 tsp tomato ketchup

Preheat oven to 200°C | **Line a baking tray** | **Microwavable plate, optional** | **Fine grater or Microplane** | **Large frying pan** | **Rolling pin or clean, dry wine bottle** | **Pastry brush**

Put your sausages on a microwavable plate and put the plate in the microwave | If they are frozen, cook on high for 90 seconds, if they're not frozen, cook for 20 seconds | Take out of the microwave and mash with a fork | Alternatively, defrost the sausages in the fridge overnight, put them in the oven for 5 minutes and mash with a fork

Peel and grate the garlic | Peel the ginger by scraping off the skin with a spoon, then grate | Thinly slice the spring onions | Finely chop the tomatoes | Remove the leaves from the thyme if the stem is woody, then chop finely

Place the frying pan over a medium heat and add the oil | Add the minced sausage and fry, stirring constantly, for 4–5 minutes, until beginning to colour | Add the spring onions and stir for 2 minutes | Add the garlic and ginger and stir for 2 minutes | Add the soy sauce, thyme, allspice, black pepper, hot sauce and ketchup and stir for 2 minutes | Pour the tomatoes into the pan and stir for 2–3 minutes, until half the liquid has evaporated | Take off the heat and leave to cool to room temperature

Put the dairy-free butter into a mixing bowl and sprinkle over the flour, turmeric and salt | Rub between your fingers to make a dry, crumbly mixture | Add the water and work it into the butter mixture with your fingers to make a dough

Divide the dough into 6 equal pieces, about 55g each | Dust a clean work surface with flour | Roll the dough pieces into thin ovals about 20cm long, 15cm wide and 3mm thick | Spoon the filling into the centre of each pastry oval | Brush round the edges with water and fold over lengthways | Crimp round the edges with a fork to seal and prick holes in the tops with a fork | Put on the baking sheet and refrigerate for 15 minutes

Take the sheet out of the fridge | Brush the patties lightly with plant-based milk

Put the sheet in the oven and bake for 20 minutes, until firm to the touch | Leave to cool slightly, then serve

TEXAN POTATO SALAD

This deliciously satisfying salad was the brainchild of our friend Sophie Pryn when she whipped up a deliciously fresh accompaniment to our Wild West Wings on page 160. It's great the next day too, so pack any leftovers into a lunchbox. You can replace the potatoes with sweet potatoes, just cook them for a bit less time.

SERVES 6—8

900g new potatoes
2 celery sticks
1 red pepper
8 spring onions
8 small pickled gherkins
4 tbsp capers
1 lemon
10g fresh dill
10g fresh parsley
10g fresh mint
10g fresh coriander
125g egg-free mayonnaise
¾ tsp salt, plus extra

Large saucepan

Put the potatoes in the pan, fill it with water and sprinkle in a generous pinch of salt | Turn on the heat to high, bring to the boil and cook for 15—20 minutes, until tender

Prep the rest of the veg | Thinly slice the celery | Cut the pepper in half, cut out the stem and seeds and dice the flesh | Trim and thinly slice the spring onions | Slice the gherkins | Finely chop the capers | Zest the lemon | Put all the prepared vegetables in a large mixing bowl with the lemon zest | Cut the lemon in half and squeeze the juice into the bowl, catching any pips in your other hand

Separate the herb leaves from any tough stems and finely chop | Add three quarters of the chopped herbs to the bowl, reserving the rest | Add the egg-free mayo and ¾ teaspoon salt to the bowl and fold everything together

Once the potatoes are cooked, drain them in a colander and run them under cold water until cool enough to handle | Cut into quarters

Add the potatoes to the mixing bowl and fold everything together | Sprinkle over the reserved herbs and serve

CRUNCHY CALI SLAW

Short and sharp, this slaw is quick to make and easy to enjoy.
You can really use anything you have leftover in your fridge
– celery, peppers, radishes, pears, beansprouts, spring onions…
It's perfect for a BBQ or to serve alongside American-style
dishes like our Wild West Wings (see page 160)
or Party Poppers (see page 165).

SERVES 6 AS A SIDE

50g almonds
1 white cabbage (about 350g shredded
    weight)
2 medium red onions
3 carrots
2 Gala or other crisp, sweet apples
15g flat-leaf parsley

FOR THE DRESSING
3 limes
200g egg-free mayonnaise
2 tbsp BBQ sauce
1 heaped tbsp mustard
½ tsp hot sauce
2 tsp salt
1 tsp black pepper
a good pinch of cayenne pepper

Preheat oven to 180°C | **Baking tray** | **Large serving bowl** | **Grater**

Spread the almonds out on the baking tray | Put the tray in the oven for 8 minutes

Cut the cabbage into quarters, discarding the core, and shred finely | Transfer to a large serving bowl, separating the shreds with your fingers

Peel and thinly slice the onions | Scatter into the bowl, separating the slices, and toss together with your hands

Peel the carrots and grate them using the large holes of a grater (or cut them into fine ribbons) | Add to the bowl and toss to mix

Core, halve and chop the apples into matchsticks and toss them into the bowl

Pick and roughly chop the parsley leaves | Add most to the bowl, reserving a small handful for garnish

Take the almonds out of the oven, spread them out on a chopping board and roughly chop into small pieces

Make the dressing | Halve the limes and squeeze the juice into a small bowl | Add the rest of the dressing ingredients and mix with a fork until smooth

Pour the dressing over the slaw and mix everything together | Sprinkle over the reserved parsley and chopped almonds and serve

DOUBLE-COOKED ROSEMARY CHIPS WITH QUICK AIOLI

Potatoes are life. We like to double-cook our chips to make them taste perfect and crispy, pairing them with a simple rosemary salt. Make double or triple batches and freeze them (once chilled) so they're ready whenever you want them.

SERVES 4

4 large Maris Piper or other floury
    potatoes (about 10–13cm long
    and 1kg in weight)
2 sprigs fresh rosemary leaves
1 tsp coarse sea salt, plus a little extra
1 tsp black pepper
2 litres cold water
2 litres rapeseed oil, for deep-frying

FOR THE QUICK AIOLI
4 tbsp egg-free mayonnaise
½ garlic clove
salt

Microplane or fine grater | **Pestle and mortar** | **Large saucepan** | **Cooling rack set over a baking tray** | **Deep-fat fryer, optional** | **Cooking thermometer**

Peel the long sides of the potatoes, leaving the ends with the skin on | Cut them into 1cm-thick slices first, then into 1cm sticks

Fill a large bowl (or the sink) with cold water | Rinse the potatoes, submerge them and leave to soak for 30 minutes

Remove the leaves from the rosemary by running your thumb and forefinger from the top to the base of the stems (the leaves should easily come away) | Finely chop and add to a pestle and mortar with the sea salt and black pepper | Grind to make a rosemary salt

Fill the large saucepan with the water and add a generous pinch of salt | Add the drained, chipped potatoes | Turn on the heat to medium-high and bring to the boil | Simmer for 5–7 minutes, until barely soft | Carefully transfer to the cooling rack, put the tray in the fridge and chill for 1 hour | Clean out the pan

Meanwhile, make the aioli | Put the egg-free mayonnaise into a small bowl | Peel the garlic then use a Microplane or fine grater to grate it into the bowl and mix with a fork | Taste and season to perfection with salt

Pour the oil into the deep-fat fryer or large saucepan, making sure it comes no more than halfway up the sides of the pan, and heat to exactly 160°C | Using a slotted spoon, carefully add two spoonfuls of the chipped potatoes to the hot oil, making sure they're submerged by at least 2.5cm | Fry for 7 minutes, until golden and crispy | Remove with the slotted spoon or fryer basket, gently shaking off any excess oil | Transfer to the cooling rack to drain | Repeat to cook all the chips

Put the chips in a bowl | Sprinkle over the rosemary salt, toss to coat and serve immediately with the aioli on the side

MASH!

The humble potato, sweet potato and beetroot take centre stage here, showing us just how creamy and delicious simple ingredients can be. Each of these mash dishes is bursting with subtle, balanced, luxurious flavour, and will add both style and substance to any hearty meal, while the sweet potato and beetroot mashes will get you well on your way to eating the rainbow.

ROAST SWEET POTATO MASH

SERVES 4 AS A SIDE

1.5kg sweet potatoes
2 garlic cloves
1 tbsp olive oil, plus extra for drizzling
8 spring onions
1 fresh red chilli
100ml unsweetened plant-based milk
50g dairy-free butter
salt and black pepper

Preheat oven to 200°C | **Line a baking tray** | **Large saucepan** | **Potato masher**

Peel the sweet potatoes and chop them into 3cm chunks | Spread over the baking tray and add the garlic cloves | Drizzle with olive oil, sprinkle with salt and pepper and roast for 30 minutes

Meanwhile, peel and finely dice the spring onions | Rip the stem from the chilli, remove the seeds and finely chop | Pour 1 tablespoon oil into the saucepan and add the onion and chilli | Fry for 2 minutes, stirring, then take off the heat

Take the tray out of the oven and let cool a little | Squeeze the garlic cloves into a bowl, mash with a fork and add to the pan | Add the sweet potato, milk and dairy-free butter and mash | Taste, season with salt and pepper and serve

ROAST BEETROOT MASH

Preheat oven to 200°C | Loaf tin | Foil | Large saucepan | Liquidiser

3 raw beetroot

1kg Maris Piper or other floury potatoes

2 garlic cloves

6 sprigs fresh thyme

2 tbsp water

2 tbsp olive oil

½ tsp salt, plus a little extra

½ tsp black pepper, plus a little extra

½ tsp chilli flakes

60g dairy-free butter

150ml unsweetened plant-based milk

Peel and quarter the beetroot and potatoes | Put the beetroot into the loaf tin with the garlic and thyme | Pour in the water, drizzle over the oil and sprinkle over the salt, pepper and chilli flakes | Cover the tin tightly with foil and bake for 45 minutes, or until a sharp knife glides easily into the thickest part of the beetroot

Meanwhile, put the potatoes in the pan | Cover with cold water, add a generous pinch of salt and put on a high heat | Bring to the boil and cook for 15–20 minutes, until tender | Drain and leave to dry, then tip back into the pan | Add the dairy-free butter and milk and mash until smooth

Take the tin out of the oven and leave to cool a little | Squeeze the roasted garlic into the liquidiser, add the beetroot and blend | Fold into the mashed potato | Taste, season with salt and pepper and serve

MUSTARD MASH

Large saucepan | Fine grater or Microplane | Frying pan | Potato masher

1kg Maris Piper or other floury potatoes

2 eschalion (banana) shallots

2 garlic cloves

1 tbsp olive oil

3 tbsp wholegrain mustard

20g dairy-free butter

120ml unsweetened plant-based milk

salt and black pepper

Peel the potatoes and put them in the saucepan | Cover with cold water and sprinkle in a generous pinch of salt | Put on a high heat, bring to the boil and cook for 15–20 minutes, until tender | Drain and leave to dry

Meanwhile, peel and thinly slice the shallots | Peel and grate the garlic

Put the frying pan on a medium heat and add the oil | Add the shallots and a small pinch of salt | Fry for 3–4 minutes | Add the garlic and stir for 2 minutes

Add the dry potatoes and mash roughly | Add the mustard, dairy-free butter and milk | Reduce the heat to low and continue to mash until smooth and warmed through | Taste, season with salt and pepper and serve

Pictured on pages 182–183

ROAST SWEET
POTATO MASH

ROAST BEETROOT
MASH

MUSTARD MASH

5

GREENS

Henry's favourite
Mega Mezze Platter

Ian's favourite
Thanksgiving Salad

ORANGE, FENNEL & WATERCRESS SALAD

A really refreshing salad, this works perfectly next to the tagine on page 98 or with any pasta dish. If you have a speed peeler or a mandoline, use it to create extra-thin slices of fennel. It's also a great dish to make a day ahead or pack into a lunchbox, just keep the dressing in a separate airtight container until you are about to eat.

SERVES 4–6

200g sourdough bread
3 tbsp olive oil
3 oranges
2 large fennel bulbs
150g blanched almonds
100g watercress
salt and black pepper

FOR THE DRESSING
6 tbsp extra-virgin olive oil
1 tsp wholegrain mustard
1 lemon

Preheat oven to 200°C | Line 2 baking trays

Tear the bread into large chunks and spread them over one of the baking trays | Drizzle over the olive oil and sprinkle over a generous pinch each of salt and pepper (you could also sprinkle over some chopped rosemary or thyme for even more flavour) | Place the tray in the oven and cook for 5–10 minutes, turning occasionally, until just golden brown and not too crispy

Peel and segment the oranges, cutting away the pith, and place them in a salad bowl | Cut the fennel in half lengthways and then slice into very thin strips | Add to the bowl | Reserve any fronds for a garnish

Spread the almonds over the second baking sheet | Put the sheet in the oven and bake for 6–8 minutes until golden

To make the dressing, add the olive oil and mustard to a small bowl | Cut the lemon in half and squeeze in the juice, catching any pips with your other hand | Stir with a fork | Taste and season with salt and pepper

Add the watercress, almonds and croutons to the salad bowl and toss | Pour over the dressing and toss again to combine | Serve immediately, garnished with a few fennel fronds if you like

THANKSGIVING SALAD

This is one of those rare, hearty salads better suited to cooler times of year. For extra points use seasonal pumpkins or squashes or try it with broccoli or cauliflower. It's great alongside Christmas dinner leftovers too, with cranberry sauce. You can roast the veg in advance: store it in the fridge and let it reach room temperature before you make the salad.

SERVES 4

100g pecans
200g cavolo nero or kale
2 x 250g bags ready-to-eat puy lentils
75g dried cranberries

FOR THE ROASTED SQUASH
1 small butternut squash (about 500–750g)
2 tbsp olive oil
1 tsp chilli flakes
salt and black pepper

FOR THE DRESSING
1 small garlic clove
1 tbsp Dijon mustard
4 tsp maple syrup
2 tbsp apple cider vinegar
6 tbsp extra-virgin olive oil
salt and black pepper

Preheat oven to 180°C | **Line 2 baking trays** | **Fine grater or Microplane** | **Jam jar with a lid** | **Kettle boiled**

Start with the roasted squash | Peel the butternut squash, cut it in half and scoop out the seeds | Cut the halves lengthways to make 2.5cm-wide strips | Lay the strips on a baking tray, drizzle over the olive oil and sprinkle with the chilli flakes | Lightly season with salt and pepper | Put the tray in the oven and bake the squash for 40 minutes, turning the pieces halfway through

Spread the pecans out on the second baking tray | Put the tray in the oven and toast for 10 minutes | Remove from the oven and set to one side

Meanwhile, make the dressing | Peel and finely grate the garlic clove | Put the Dijon mustard, maple syrup, apple cider vinegar, olive oil and grated garlic in the jar, put the lid on and shake vigorously to combine | Taste and season to perfection with salt and pepper

Trim and discard the tough stems from the cavolo nero or kale then roughly chop | Fill a mixing bowl with boiling water from the kettle | Submerge the cavolo nero or kale in the boiling water and blanch for 1 minute, until slightly soft | Drain and set aside

Pour the dressing into a large mixing bowl and tip in the lentils | Stir to evenly coat | Add the dried cranberries and fold them into the lentils

Divide the dressed lentils among bowls | Place the cavolo nero or kale and squash on top | Scatter over the toasted pecans and serve immediately

SPICY THAI SALAD

There are so many amazing flavours working together here with oodles of fresh herbs, sweet mango and a perfectly balanced chilli-satay dressing. Double-batch the sauce to serve as a dip for spring rolls or to add a Thai taste to any salad or greens.

SERVES 4

½ cucumber
2 baby pak choi
¼ small red cabbage (about 180g)
1 red pepper
1 carrot
2 spring onions
1 ripe mango
10g fresh mint leaves
15g fresh coriander leaves
4 tbsp peanuts
2 limes

FOR THE SAUCE
2 limes
2 garlic cloves
4cm piece fresh ginger
2 tbsp caster sugar
2 tbsp sriracha
3 tsp sesame oil
2 tsp olive oil
4 tbsp soy sauce
10g fresh coriander leaves
140g smooth peanut butter
4 tbsp water

Peeler | Liquidiser | Pestle and mortar, optional

First prep the vegetables, mango and herbs for your salad | Halve the cucumber lengthways and cut it into ribbons using a vegetable peeler | Trim and shred the pak choi and red cabbage | Cut the pepper in half, cut out the stem and seeds and cut into thin strips | Peel the carrot and peel into ribbons | Trim the spring onions and cut them lengthways into thin strips | Slice the mango lengthways down either side of the stone, spoon out the flesh and cut into thin strips | Chop the mint and coriander leaves

Put all the prepped ingredients into a large mixing bowl and gently toss with your hands so they're well mixed

Now make the sauce | Cut the limes in half and squeeze the juice into the liquidiser | Peel and roughly chop the garlic | Peel the ginger by scraping off the skin with a spoon and chop roughly | Add the garlic and ginger to the liquidiser along with the sugar, sriracha, sesame oil, olive oil, soy sauce, coriander leaves, peanut butter and water | Blend to a smooth sauce | Pour into a serving jug

Crush the peanuts in a mortar or with the end of a rolling pin | Cut the limes into wedges | Divide the salad among bowls, drizzle over a generous helping of the sauce and sprinkle over the broken peanuts | Serve with 2 lime wedges each

SPINACH & RICOTTA ZUCCHINIOLI

This wonderfully fresh dish was inspired by Matthew Kenney's raw lasagne. Little ravioli-like parcels are filled with a velvety cashew cream. Make double the amount of pesto and save half to serve with pasta; it will keep in an airtight container in the fridge for up to 3 days. To save time, you could use a good-quality shop-bought dairy-free pesto instead.

SERVES 4

225g cashews
1 red onion
2 garlic cloves
2 courgettes
100g dairy-free cheese
100g fresh spinach
30g fresh basil
1 lemon
200ml water
1 tsp salt, plus a little extra
6 tbsp nutritional yeast
2 tbsp olive oil
100g cherry tomatoes
50g rocket
black pepper

FOR THE PESTO
50g fresh basil
1 garlic clove
1 lemon
100g shop-bought toasted pine nuts
150ml extra-virgin olive oil, plus extra for drizzling
¼ tsp salt
1 tbsp nutritional yeast

Medium saucepan of boiling water on a high heat | **Peeler** | **Grater** | **Liquidiser** | **Frying pan**

Tip the cashews into the pan of hot water and boil for 20 minutes, until soft

Meanwhile, get your other ingredients ready | Peel and dice the onion and garlic | Trim the courgettes and peel into at least 32 long, thin ribbons | Grate the dairy-free cheese | Roughly chop the spinach | Pick the basil leaves and chop roughly

Drain the cashews and tip them into the liquidiser | Cut the lemon in half and squeeze in the juice, catching any pips in your other hand | Add the water, 1 teaspoon salt and the nutritional yeast | Blend to a smooth, thick cream

Put the frying pan over a medium heat | Pour in the olive oil | When the pan is hot, add the onion and cook for 5 minutes until soft | Add the garlic and stir for 2 minutes | Add the cashew cream and dairy-free cheese and stir until melted | Add the chopped spinach and basil and cook for 3 minutes, until wilted | Taste and season | Remove from the heat and leave to cool to room temperature | You should have a really thick mixture

To make your zucchinioli parcels, lay two courgette ribbons on a clean surface so that they slightly overlap lengthways | Lay two more ribbons across them, slightly overlapping, to make a large cross shape with two vertical and two horizontal ribbons | Spoon 2–3 tablespoons of the ricotta cream into the centre of the cross | Fold the courgette over the filling to make a neat little parcel | Repeat to make eight zucchinioli

To make the pesto, clean out the liquidiser | Pluck the basil leaves and discard the stems | Peel the garlic | Add both to the liquidiser | Cut the lemon in half and squeeze the juice into the liquidiser, catching any pips with your other hand | Add the pine nuts, extra-virgin olive oil, salt and nutritional yeast | Pulse to a pesto consistency

Plate up! | Halve the tomatoes | Divide the rocket and tomatoes among plates | Drizzle over a little extra-virgin olive oil | Flip over the zucchinioli and place them on the plates, drizzling with a touch more oil | Sprinkle with a little salt | Spoon pesto over each portion and serve immediately

MEGA MEZZE PLATTER

The flavours on these sharing plates are second to none.
This mezze will wow your guests and they will all be eating
and smiling and laughing, and we promise it will be worth
the effort! If you're feeling extra adventurous, try adding the
Falafels from page 78 and the Tzatziki from page 58. You can
even make your own flatbreads using the recipe on page 78
— make the thinner versions, which are better for dipping.

SERVES 6

1 x portion Baba Ganoush (see page 197)
1 x portion Lemon & Coriander Hummus
   (see page 196)
1 x portion Kofta (see opposite)
1 x portion Batata Harra (see page 196)
1 x portion Tabbouleh (see opposite)
6 pitta breads or flatbreads
200g olives
a handful of small cornichons (or use
   our Quick Red Onion Pickle,
   see page 107)

Preheat oven to 180°C | Grill on high heat | Line 2 large baking trays
with foil | Food processor | Large frying pan | Salad spinner or colander
| Clean tea towel | Large saucepan

Start by getting the aubergines under the grill for the **Baba Ganoush**

Next make the **Lemon & Coriander Hummus**

Then make the **Tabbouleh**

Take the aubergines out of the oven and set aside until you're ready to
make the **Baba Ganoush**

Now make the **Kofta** | Once cooked, open the oven door and let the heat
lower to 100°C | Put the cooked kofta back in the oven to keep warm

Make the **Batata Harra** and put them in the oven to keep warm

Put the pitta breads in the oven to warm through

Finish making your **Baba Ganoush**

Lay out your mezze dishes and serve

Pictured on pages 198–199

KOFTA

MAKES 18

2 courgettes
1 large red onion
3 large garlic cloves
30g fresh parsley
30g fresh coriander
2 tbsp olive oil
1 tbsp ground cumin
1 tsp ground coriander
½ tsp chilli powder
½ tsp ground cinnamon
2 x 400g tins chickpeas
200g dried breadcrumbs
1 lemon
salt and black pepper

Preheat oven to 180°C | Grater | Clean tea towel | Fine grater or Microplane | Frying pan | Food processor | Line a large baking tray

Coarsely grate the courgette into a bowl | Sprinkle with a pinch of salt and stir to mix | Set aside for 10 minutes | Wrap the grated courgette in a clean tea towel and twist tightly to squeeze out the water

Peel and finely chop the red onion | Peel and finely grate the garlic | Pick the leaves from the parsley and coriander and discard the stems

Place the frying pan over a medium heat and add the oil | Add the onion and fry for 7 minutes, until translucent | Add the garlic and stir for 1 minute | Add the cumin, ground coriander, chilli powder and cinnamon and stir them into the onion | Add the grated courgette, stir for 1–2 minutes and take the pan off the heat

Pour the contents of the pan into the food processor | Drain and rinse the chickpeas and add to the processor along with the breadcrumbs, chopped parsley, and coriander | Cut the lemon in half and squeeze in the juice, catching any pips in your other hand | Blitz to a textured dough | Take the lid off, remove the blade, taste and season with salt and pepper, stirring them in with a spoon

Split the mixture into 18 pieces (about 60g each) and roll between your palms to make long oval shapes | Spread over the baking tray | Put the tray in the oven and bake for 20 minutes, until cooked through and crisping at the edges | Remove and serve immediately

TABBOULEH

SERVES 6

100g bulgur wheat
4 tbsp olive oil
1½ tsp salt
175ml boiling water
16 cherry tomatoes
1 medium cucumber
200g fresh flat-leaf parsley
15 fresh mint leaves
4 spring onions
3 lemons
½ tsp maple syrup
2 tbsp mixed seeds

Kettle boiled

First cook the bulgur wheat | Put the bulgur wheat, 1 tablespoon of the olive oil and ½ teaspoon of salt into a heatproof mixing bowl | Pour over the boiling water, put a dinner plate on top and set aside for 30 minutes | Remove the plate, fluff up the bulgur wheat with a fork and leave to cool to room temperature

Meanwhile, get the rest of the ingredients ready | Quarter the tomatoes | Chop the cucumber into 5mm cubes | Rip the leaves from the parsley and finely chop, discarding the stems | Finely chop the mint and spring onions | Add the chopped veg and herbs to the bowl | Cut the lemons in half and squeeze in the juice, catching any pips in your other hand | Add the remaining olive oil and salt, the maple syrup and mixed seeds | Tip in the bulgur wheat and fold it into the rest of the ingredients before serving

BATATA HARRA (SPICY POTATOES)

SERVES 6

Large saucepan | Fine grater or Microplane | Large frying pan

1kg Maris Piper or other
    floury potatoes
1 small red onion
3 garlic cloves
20g fresh parsley
20g fresh dill
5 tbsp olive oil
2 tsp chilli flakes
2 tsp ground coriander
2 tsp ground turmeric
1 lemon
salt and black pepper

Peel the potatoes and cut them into 3-3.5cm chunks | Put them in the saucepan and cover with cold water | Put the pan over a high heat, bring to the boil and cook for 12–15 minutes | Take the pan off the heat and tip the potatoes into a colander | Leave to steam dry for 10 minutes

Meanwhile, peel and finely dice the red onion | Peel and grate the garlic | Pick the leaves from the parsley and discard the stems | Finely chop the dill and parsley

Place the frying pan over a medium heat and add the oil | Add the onion and stir for 3 minutes, until soft | Add the garlic and stir for 1 minute | Reduce the heat slightly and stir in the chilli flakes, ground coriander and turmeric | Cut the lemon in half and squeeze in the juice, catching any pips with your other hand | Toss the potatoes in the colander to roughen the edges and add them to the frying pan | Turn the heat back up to medium and cook for 15 minutes, gently stirring the potatoes around in the pan occasionally to make sure they're well coated, golden and have started to crisp up at the edges | Stir in the chopped herbs and salt and pepper to taste | Serve immediately

LEMON & CORIANDER HUMMUS

MAKES 400g

Food processor

1 lemon
1 x 400g tin chickpeas
1 small garlic clove
2 tbsp tahini
¾ tsp salt, plus more to taste
4 tbsp water
2 tbsp olive oil
10g fresh coriander
black pepper, to taste

Cut the lemon in half and squeeze the juice into the food processor, catching any pips with your other hand | Drain and rinse the chickpeas | Peel the garlic

In a food processor, blitz the chickpeas, garlic, tahini, salt, water and olive oil | Remove the blade

Pick the leaves from the coriander and discard the stems | Stir the leaves into the hummus

Taste and season to perfection with salt and pepper, transfer to a bowl and serve immediately

BABA GANOUSH

MAKES 500g

3 medium aubergines (about 900g)
3 garlic cloves
1 lemon
3 tbsp tahini
80ml + 1 tbsp extra-virgin olive oil
15g fresh parsley leaves
a few pomegranate seeds, optional
salt

Grill on high heat | **Line a baking tray with foil** | **Salad spinner or colander** | **Fine grater or Microplane**

Place the whole aubergines on the lined baking tray | Put the tray on the top shelf of the grill | Grill for 1 hour, turning occasionally, until very, very tender | Remove the tray from the grill | Pull up the foil around the aubergines and seal the top to make a package | Leave to steam for 10 minutes (or until you're ready to make the baba ganoush)

Open the foil and, when cool enough to handle, slice each aubergine in half lengthways | Scoop the flesh into a salad spinner or colander | Spin gently to remove all the moisture, or gently press the aubergine in the colander until most of the liquid has dripped out | Transfer to a mixing bowl

Now combine with the rest of the ingredients | Peel and grate the garlic into the bowl | Cut the lemon in half and squeeze in the juice, catching any pips with your other hand | Stir vigorously for 2 minutes until you have a paste | Stir in the tahini | Slowly add the 80ml olive oil, stirring continuously to allow the mixture to emulsify and become really creamy | Season generously with salt | Taste and add more lemon juice if necessary | Roughly chop the parsley and add most to the bowl, stirring it in

Transfer to a serving dish | Make a small well in the middle and pour in 1 tablespoon olive oil | Garnish with a few more parsley leaves and a handful of pomegranate seeds, if using, and serve

BANG BANG NOODLE SALAD

One of our most epic salads, this dish tastes like a takeaway but has all the goodness of a salad. Bangin' veg with an incredible Asian dressing, you'll want to make it again and again. Try the dressing with roasted veggies or any Asian- or Thai-flavoured meal. Switch out the rice noodles with soba noodles for a higher protein meal or add some griddled tofu.

SERVES 3–4

100g dried rice vermicelli
4 tbsp sesame oil
¼ cucumber
1 carrot
1 red pepper
1 head pak choi
3 spring onions
3 tbsp peanuts
1 fresh red chilli
10g fresh coriander
7.5cm piece fresh ginger
2 limes
1½ tsp chilli flakes
4 tbsp peanut butter
2 tbsp soy sauce
3 tsp maple syrup
4 tbsp water
4 portobello mushrooms
1 tbsp vegetable oil

Kettle boiled | Peeler | Saucepan | Food processor | Wok

Prep the vermicelli | Pour the boiling water into a large mixing bowl | Submerge the vermicelli in the hot water and leave them to soak for 5 minutes (or follow the instructions on the packet) | Drain the noodles through a sieve and run them under cold water until cool | Tip them back into the bowl | Pour over 1 tablespoon of the sesame oil, toss to coat and set to one side

Now make the salad | Peel the cucumber into ribbons using a vegetable peeler, discarding the watery middle | Trim and peel the carrot, then peel it into ribbons | Cut the pepper in half, cut out the stem and seeds and slice into long, thin strips | Cut out the thick stem off the pak choi and shred the leaves thinly | Trim the spring onions, cut them in half and then thinly slice them lengthways | Roughly chop or crush the peanuts | Rip off the stem from the chilli and cut it into thin slices | Pick the coriander leaves and discard the stems

Add the vegetables and herbs you've just prepared to the bowl with the noodles | Toss everything together to combine | Divide between bowls and set to one side

Quickly make the dressing | Peel the ginger by scraping off the skin with a spoon and roughly chop | Zest one of the limes | Cut both limes in half and squeeze the juice into the food processor | Add the lime zest, peeled ginger, 2 tablespoons of the sesame oil, the chilli flakes, peanut butter, soy sauce, maple syrup and water | Blitz to make a sauce

Cut the portobello mushrooms into thin strips | Put the wok over a high heat and add the vegetable oil and remaining sesame oil | When the pan is hot, add the mushrooms and fry for 5–6 minutes, until they shrink in size and darken in colour

Divide the cooked mushrooms among the bowls | Drizzle over the spicy peanut dressing | Sprinkle over the broken peanuts and sliced red chilli and serve immediately

ROMESCO SALAD

We love Barcelona and this dish whisks us away to the wonderful beachfront. We definitely recommend making double the sauce and keeping some for dressing another salad, or for dipping nachos or crudités – and if you like it spicy you could certainly add a little more heat.

SERVES 4

about 300g bread (e.g. sourdough)
2 tbsp olive oil
250g mixed or cherry tomatoes
30g blanched almonds
30g hazelnuts
1 x 350g jar roasted peppers (or you can make your own by roasting the peppers at 200°C until blackened, then cooling in a bag and peeling)
4 spring onions
a small bunch of fresh parsley
60g rocket or peppery salad leaves such as lamb's lettuce or mizuna
salt and black pepper

FOR THE DRESSING
45g flaked almonds
2 garlic cloves
1 roasted red pepper from the jar for the salad (about 100g)
70g tomato purée
10g fresh flat-leaf parsley
1 tsp smoked paprika
¼ tsp cayenne pepper
2 tbsp red wine vinegar
80ml extra-virgin olive oil
salt and black pepper

Preheat oven to 180°C | Line 2 baking trays | Food processor

Remove the crusts from the bread, then cut it into 1cm croutons | Scatter over a baking tray and drizzle with the olive oil | Sprinkle over generous pinches of salt and pepper | Put the tray in the oven for 12 minutes, turning the croutons halfway through | Remove when golden and crispy

To make the dressing, spread the flaked almonds over the second baking tray | Put the tray in the oven for 5 minutes, until the almonds are golden brown | Tip into the food processor along with all the dressing ingredients except for the olive oil, salt and pepper | Blitz until smooth, scraping down the sides of the bowl with a spatula if necessary to combine all the ingredients | While the processor is running, slowly add the olive oil until you have a smooth dressing | Taste and season with salt and pepper | Pour into a serving dish and clean out the food processor

Cut the tomatoes into bite-sized pieces | Tip the blanched almonds and hazelnuts into the clean food processor and pulse to chop roughly | Cut the roasted peppers into 3cm pieces | Trim and thinly slice the spring onions

To assemble the salad, add the tomatoes, parsley, peppers, spring onions and salad leaves to a large bowl | Sprinkle over the chopped nuts and croutons | Serve in the bowl and toss together at the table just before serving, with the dressing on the side for people to help themselves

CRUNCHY CARNIVAL SALAD

This spicy and sweet salad brings together all our favourite flavours from the famous Notting Hill Carnival – great for a relaxed healthy lunch on a sunny day. Make extra to pack into a lunchbox. It also goes really well with griddled tofu or jackfruit roasted in a spicy jerk or BBQ sauce.

SERVES 6

30g fresh coriander
¼ red cabbage
8 spring onions
2 carrots
1 red pepper
2 mangoes
1 avocado
1 large fresh red chilli
50g egg-free mayonnaise
1 tsp–1 tbsp Encona West Indian
   hot sauce
1 tsp maple syrup
2 limes
200g sweetcorn
salt and black pepper

FOR THE SWEET POTATOES
2 large sweet potatoes (about 675g)
1 tbsp olive oil
½ tbsp chilli flakes
salt and black pepper

FOR THE RICE & BEANS
5 sprigs fresh thyme
2 garlic cloves
1 x 400g tin kidney beans
1 x 400ml tin full-fat coconut milk
100ml water
¼ tsp ground allspice
1 tsp salt
¼ tsp black pepper
200g long-grain rice

Preheat oven to 180°C | Baking tray | String | Medium saucepan

First cook the sweet potatoes | Peel the sweet potatoes and cut them into 2cm chunks | Spread over the baking tray | Sprinkle over the oil, chilli flakes and a little seasoning | Roast for 25–30 minutes, turning halfway

Meanwhile, make the rice and beans | Pick and roughly chop the coriander leaves and set aside | Tie the coriander stems and thyme together with string to make a bouquet garni | Peel the garlic | Drain the kidney beans

Put the saucepan over a medium heat | Add the coconut milk, water, allspice, salt, pepper, garlic and bouquet garni and bring to a simmer | Wash the rice under cold water until it runs clear and tip into the saucepan | Stir, reduce the heat to a very gentle simmer, put the lid on and cook until all the liquid has been absorbed, about 13–16 minutes | Take the pan off the heat | Remove the garlic and bouquet garni | Fold in the kidney beans | Put the lid back on for 5 minutes

Prep the rest of the fresh ingredients | Shred the cabbage | Cut the spring onions in half and shred them lengthways | Peel the carrots and then peel them into ribbons | Trim the pepper and slice into thin strips | Slice the mango lengthways down either side of the stone, spoon out the flesh and slice thinly | Halve and carefully stone the avocados by tapping the stone firmly with the heel of a knife so that it lodges in the stone, then twist and remove | Scoop out the flesh, then slice thinly | Rip the stem from the chilli, cut it in half, scrape out the seeds and slice thinly

Put the egg-free mayonnaise, hot sauce and maple syrup into a large bowl | Halve one of the limes, squeeze in the juice and stir to mix | Add the cabbage, spring onions, carrots, pepper, chilli, coriander leaves and sweetcorn | Toss to coat in the dressing

Serve the rice into large bowls | Spoon over the roasted sweet potatoes | Pile over the salad and top with the avocado and mango slices | Squeeze more lime over the avocado | Quarter the remaining lime and place a wedge on each bowl | Serve immediately

HEALTHY MEAL PREP

A wholefoods, plant-based diet is a really healthy way to live your life and with a little bit of planning it's easy to fit it into your lifestyle. We love to prep healthy meals so that we can grab a meal and go. We prefer to do this a couple of days in advance (rather than making 7 days-worth of meals in one go) so that the food tastes deliciously fresh when you eat it. See page 24 for more on meal planning and meal prep.

On the following pages are three easy and tasty recipes that will give you enough meals for two full days. This meal plan is nutritionally balanced with lots of green veg and plenty of colour to make sure you get loads of plant-filled energy in your diet — we suggest adding a banana for a snack each day too. And we've broken them down so that you know exactly what to prep and when. See how the meal plan looks on pages 210—211.

GREEN BREAKFAST SMOOTHIES

This smoothie is a fantastic way to fill your body with healthy veg and green is king here. If you pack your diet with greens first thing in the morning it helps you get a head-start on a healthy day. Each smoothie is about 700ml, which is a lot! You can drink half in the morning and take the rest with you in a bottle for an afternoon snack.

MAKES BREAKFAST AND
A SNACK FOR 2 DAYS

2 bananas
2 apples
120g frozen mixed berries
60g mixed nuts
2 tbsp ground flaxseed
150g kale
100g spinach
300ml B12-fortified unsweetened
   plant-based milk
300ml water
4 tbsp plant-based protein powder,
   optional

The night before | 2 freezer-proof containers or bags

Peel and roughly chop the bananas | Roughly chop the apple | Divide between the freezer-proof containers along with all the berries, nuts and seeds | Place in the freezer and leave overnight

In the morning | Liquidiser

Place half the kale and half the spinach into the liquidiser with half the milk, half the water and half the protein powder, if using | Blitz until completely smooth | Take one of the containers out of the freezer and add the contents to the liquidiser | Blend until smooth, then drink the whole thing for breakfast or transfer to a portable container to drink throughout the day (give it a little shake before drinking as it may have separated)

PIRI PIRI PROTEIN LUNCHBOX

This lunchbox is tasty, healthy and packed full of protein. The tofu is flavoured with delicious chilli sauce and the rice and peas complement it perfectly, while everything is brought together by a wholesome turmeric hummus. You could use shop-bought hummus and chilli sauce for speed. However, our Home-Made Sambal Chilli Sauce and Turmeric Hummus (see page 208) are simply incredible and worth the extra time on prep day.

MAKES LUNCH FOR 2 DAYS

2 x 280g blocks tofu
240g kidney or other beans from a tin
1 x 250g pack of cooked brown rice
20g fresh coriander
50g fresh spinach
1 tsp olive oil
2 tsp chilli sauce (shop-bought or use our Home-Made Sambal Chilli Sauce, see page 208)
80g Tenderstem broccoli
½ lemon
½ lime
salt and black pepper

FOR THE QUICK TURMERIC HUMMUS
(or use our Home-Made Turmeric Hummus, see page 208)
230g shop-bought hummus
1 tsp ground turmeric
½ tsp cayenne pepper

FOR THE QUICK CHILLI MARINADE
(or use our Home-Made Sambal Chilli Sauce, see page 208)
75ml good-quality low-sugar chilli sauce (we use Cholula)
1 tsp olive oil

The night before | Tofu press or 2 clean tea towels and a weight such as a heavy book | Griddle pan

Press the tofu using a tofu press or place it between two clean tea towels, lay it on a plate and put a weight on top | Leave for 30 minutes to drain and firm up

Make the chilli marinade by pouring the chilli sauce and olive oil into a bowl and mixing with a fork (or follow the recipe on page 208) | Slice the tofu into 1cm-thick slices and add them to the marinade | Leave for 10 minutes

Make the turmeric hummus by putting the hummus, turmeric and cayenne into a bowl and mixing until completely combined (or follow the recipe on page 208)

Drain the kidney beans and put them into a bowl with the rice | Roughly chop the coriander and spinach and add them to the bowl | Add the olive oil and chilli sauce | Stir everything together | Taste and season to perfection

Put the griddle pan on a high heat | When it's really hot, add the tofu slices and leave to cook for 3–4 minutes without moving them so they develop distinct, solid char lines | Turn and repeat on the other side | Remove the tofu but leave the pan on the heat

Add the broccoli to the pan and leave to cook for about 4 minutes, until they have char lines underneath | Turn and repeat on the other side | When the broccoli are softened with nice char lines all over, transfer to a plate | Squeeze over the juice of the half lemon, catching any pips in your other hand

Divide the rice and beans, griddled tofu, broccoli and hummus between the two containers | Quarter the half lime and put 2 pieces in each box | Refrigerate

In the morning | Don't forget to take your lunchbox with you to work!

Squeeze the lime over your delicious, healthy lunch and enjoy!

HOME-MADE SAMBAL CHILLI SAUCE

MAKES 190g

1–2 garlic cloves
2–3 eschalion (banana) shallots
   (about 100g)
2 fresh chillies
2cm piece fresh ginger
1 lemon
1–2 roasted red peppers from a jar
   (about 100g)
½ tsp ground turmeric
1 tbsp oil
60ml white wine vinegar
salt and black pepper

Liquidiser | Wok or frying pan

Peel the garlic and shallots | Rip the stems from the chillies | Peel the ginger by scraping off the skin with a spoon | Zest half the lemon into the liquidiser | Add all the ingredients except the vinegar, oil and lemon to the liquidiser and blend to a paste

Place the wok or frying pan on a medium-high heat and add the oil | When it's hot, add the paste, reduce to a low heat and cook for about 15 minutes, stirring regularly so it doesn't stick | Add the white wine vinegar | Cut the lemon in half and squeeze in the juice, catching any pips in your other hand | Stir everything together and remove from the heat | Taste and season to perfection

HOME-MADE TURMERIC HUMMUS

MAKES 300g,
OR 2 PORTIONS

1 x 400g tin chickpeas
2 small garlic cloves
1 lemon
1 tsp ground turmeric
1 tsp ground ginger
¾ tsp salt
½ tsp cayenne pepper
4 tbsp water
2 tbsp tahini
2 tbsp olive oil

Food processor

Drain the chickpeas and save the water (aquafaba) for another recipe | Peel the garlic | Cut the lemon in half and squeeze the juice into the food processor, catching the pips with your other hand | Put all the remaining ingredients into the food processor | Blitz to a smooth paste

EASY TOMATO PASTA WITH GRIDDLED GREENS

This cheeky little pasta dish is so quick to rustle up in the evening. We use wholewheat pasta as it is higher in fibre. It's a great recipe for batch cooking – make multiple helpings of the sauce and store it in the freezer for up to a month.

MAKES DINNER FOR 2 DAYS

PREP
30g fresh parsley
1 medium onion
2 garlic cloves
1 red pepper (about 100g)
1 medium carrot
1 tbsp olive oil
1 x 400g tin chopped tomatoes
400ml water
1–2 tsp chilli sauce
¼ tsp dried oregano
½ tsp chilli flakes
1 tbsp nutritional yeast, optional
salt and black pepper

FOR EACH SERVING
100–110g dried wholewheat pasta
50g asparagus
1 tsp olive oil
½ lemon
30g mixed salad greens, to serve
salt

The night before | Fine grater or Microplane | Food processor | Medium saucepan | 2 x airtight containers

. . . .

Remove the leaves from the parsley and place them in the fridge either in an airtight container or on top of some kitchen paper

Peel the onion | Peel and grate the garlic | Cut the pepper in half and cut out the stem and seeds | Trim the carrot | Put the parsley stems, onion, carrot and pepper into the food processor and blitz until finely chopped

Put the saucepan on a medium heat and pour in the oil | Tip the chopped vegetables from the food processor into the pan and sauté for 8 minutes, stirring | Add the garlic and sauté for 2 minutes | Add the chopped tomatoes, water, 1 teaspoon chilli sauce, the oregano and the chilli flakes | Taste and season to perfection, adding more chilli sauce if you like | Simmer for 10 minutes, until the sauce is thick | Add the nutritional yeast, if using | Divide between the containers, leave to cool and then refrigerate

The next day | Large saucepan of boiling salted water on a high heat | Griddle pan on a high heat | Small saucepan, optional

. . . .

Add the pasta to the pan of boiling salted water | Cook following the instructions on the packet, drain and tip back into the pan

Meanwhile, rub the asparagus spears with the oil and lay the spears across the lines of the hot griddle pan | Cook for about 5 minutes without moving the spears, until they have black char lines | Turn them over and repeat | Cut the lemon in half | Finish the asparagus with a sprinkling of salt and squeeze over the juice of half the lemon, catching any pips in your other hand

Take one of the sauce containers from the fridge and reheat the pasta sauce on the hob or in the microwave, until piping hot | Take out half the parsley leaves and roughly chop

Add the sauce to the pasta and mix until the pasta is evenly coated | Squeeze over the some lemon juice, catching any pips | Stir in the chopped parsley leaves and mix everything together

Serve the pasta on plates with salad greens and the griddled asparagus

Repeat the following day

6

DESSERTS

Henry's favourite
Bakewell Tart

Ian's favourite
Empire Biscuits

BANANA BREAD DOUGHNUTS

These doughnuts are a fun, delightfully delicious treat and look beautiful! Get creative with the toppings – the world is your oyster. You could even play about with different icing flavours as well.

MAKES 6 LARGE OR
12 MINI DOUGHNUTS

2 small ripe bananas
  (200g peeled weight)
125g plain flour
½ tsp bicarbonate of soda
¼ tsp salt
½ tsp ground cinnamon
55g coconut oil
40g coconut sugar
30g caster sugar
30ml unsweetened plant-based milk
½ tsp apple cider vinegar
½ tsp vanilla extract
30g sultanas

FOR THE TOPPINGS
100g icing sugar
1½ tbsp warm water
a pinch of ground cinnamon
¼ tsp vanilla extract
30g pecans
15g dark chocolate

Preheat oven to 170°C | Food processor | Grease a doughnut tray | Cooling rack

Peel the bananas and put them in the food processor | Add the plain flour, bicarbonate of soda, salt, ground cinnamon, coconut oil, coconut sugar, caster sugar, milk, apple cider vinegar and vanilla extract and blitz to a smooth cream | Take off the lid and remove the blade | Pour in the sultanas and mix them into the batter with a spoon

Carefully spoon the mixture into the doughnut tray, making sure the holes are filled to the top | Put the tray in the hot oven and bake for 25 minutes until a skewer inserted into the middle comes out clean | Remove and transfer the doughnuts to a cooling rack | Leave to cool to room temperature

While the doughnuts are baking, make the toppings | Sift the icing sugar into a mixing bowl | Add the warm water, ground cinnamon and vanilla extract and stir everything together to make a thick, smooth icing

Finely chop the pecans | Grate the dark chocolate

Artfully drizzle the icing all over the doughnuts and quickly sprinkle over the pecans and chocolate | Serve immediately

We heart ice cream and you can now find bangin' dairy-free versions in the shops. But there's something magical about making your own. It's easiest with an ice-cream maker (ours costs £20). However, you can also just use a freezer and a whisk; take it out and stir it occasionally for a smooth texture. Use the basic vanilla recipe and add your own delicious flavourings! The vodka ensures you get a nice soft scoop but you can leave it out if you prefer.

CLASSIC CHOCOLATE

MAKES ABOUT 1.5kg

500g cashews
100g dark chocolate
500ml unsweetened plant-based milk
175ml light maple syrup
6 tbsp cocoa powder
¾ tsp xantham gum
1 tsp chocolate vodka
     (or just use normal vodka)

Large saucepan of boiling water on a high heat, optional | Kettle boiled | Small saucepan | Heatproof bowl | Liquidiser | Ice-cream maker or roasting dish and whisk | 2-litre freezer-proof container

....

Put the cashews in the pan of hot water and boil for 15 minutes until they are soft and have rehydrated (or soak them overnight in cold water)

Melt the chocolate | Pour hot water into the small saucepan until it's about 3cm deep and bring to the boil | Reduce the heat to a simmer | Put a heatproof bowl on top of the pan, ensuring the water doesn't touch the bottom | Break half the dark chocolate into the bowl and leave it to melt | Remove and leave to cool a little | Alternatively, melt the chocolate in the microwave in 15-second bursts

Blend all the ice-cream ingredients except for the reserved chocolate in the liquidiser until smooth | Taste and adjust with more maple syrup, cocoa and/or vodka until you're happy with the flavour

Pour into the ice-cream maker and follow the manufacturer's instructions to make delicious ice cream | Alternatively, pour into the roasting dish and put in the freezer until firm, but still pourable, removing occasionally to whisk, if you like, to improve the texture

Melt the reserved chocolate using the method above and drizzle some of it over the bottom of the freezer-proof container | Pour over a layer of ice cream and drizzle with more melted chocolate | Repeat until all the ice cream is used up, finishing with a final drizzle of chocolate | Cover and freeze | When the ice cream has expanded and frozen through, it's ready to serve

BANOFFEE WITH CARAMEL SAUCE

MAKES ABOUT 1.5kg

500g cashews
3 bananas (about 380g peeled weight)
500ml unsweetened plant-based milk
175ml maple syrup
1 tsp vanilla extract
¾ tsp xantham gum
1 tsp vodka

FOR THE CARAMEL SAUCE
200ml full-fat coconut milk
50g light soft brown sugar
50g golden caster sugar
¼ tsp sea salt
1 tsp vanilla extract

Large saucepan of boiling water on a high heat, optional | Liquidiser | Ice-cream maker or roasting dish and whisk | Medium heavy-based saucepan | 2-litre freezer-proof container

. . . .

Put the cashews in the pan of hot water and boil for 15 minutes until they are soft and have rehydrated (or soak them overnight in cold water)

Peel the bananas then blend all the ice-cream ingredients in the liquidiser until smooth | Taste and adjust the maple syrup, vanilla and/or vodka until you're happy with the flavour

Pour into the ice-cream maker and follow the manufacturer's instructions to make delicious ice cream | Alternatively, pour into the roasting dish and put in the freezer until firm but pourable, removing occasionally to whisk, if you like, to improve the texture

Meanwhile, make the caramel sauce | Place the coconut milk, sugars and salt in the medium saucepan and put over a medium-high heat | Bring to the boil, whisking constantly, and cook for 5–10 minutes, until caramelised and thickened (it will boil up in the pan, so be careful) | Remove from the heat and stir in the vanilla extract | Set aside to cool

Once the ice-cream is firm, drizzle some of the caramel into the bottom of the freezer-proof container | Cover with a layer of the just-churned ice cream | Drizzle with more caramel sauce | Repeat to use up all the ingredients | Cover and freeze

Pictured on pages 220–221

CLEAN SLATE VANILLA

MAKES ABOUT 1.5kg

500g cashews
500ml unsweetened plant-based milk
175ml light agave or maple syrup
2 tbsp vanilla paste
¾ tsp xantham gum
1 tsp vodka

Large saucepan of boiling water on a high heat, optional | Liquidiser | Ice-cream maker or roasting dish and whisk | 2-litre freezer-proof container

....

Put the cashews in the pan of hot water and boil for 15 minutes until they are soft and have rehydrated (or soak them overnight in cold water)

Blend all the ice-cream ingredients in the liquidiser until smooth | Taste and add more vanilla, syrup and/or vodka if necessary to get the flavour right

Pour into the ice-cream maker and follow the manufacturer's instructions to make delicious ice cream | Alternatively, pour into the container and put in the freezer until frozen, removing occasionally to whisk, if you like, to improve the texture

RASPBERRY RIPPLE COOKIE CRUMBLE

MAKES ABOUT 1.5kg

500g cashews
500ml unsweetened plant-based milk
175ml light agave or maple syrup
2 tbsp vanilla paste
¾ tsp xanthan gum
1 tsp vodka
154g plant-based chocolate
   sandwich cookies

FOR THE RASPBERRY SAUCE
400g raspberries
100g golden caster sugar

Large saucepan of boiling water on a high heat, optional | Liquidiser | Ice-cream maker or roasting dish and whisk | Medium saucepan | 2-litre freezer-proof container

....

Put the cashews in the pan of hot water and boil for 15 minutes until they are soft and have rehydrated (or soak them overnight in cold water)

Blend all the ice-cream ingredients in the liquidiser until smooth | Taste and add more syrup, vanilla and/or vodka until you're happy with the flavour

Pour into the ice-cream maker and follow the manufacturer's instructions to make delicious ice cream | Alternatively, pour into the roasting dish and put in the freezer until firm, but still pourable, removing occasionally to whisk, if you like, to improve the texture

Meanwhile, make the raspberry sauce | Place the raspberries and sugar in the medium saucepan and put over a medium-high heat | Cook, stirring regularly, for 10–15 minutes, until very thick | Remove from the heat and push through a sieve to remove the seeds | Set aside and allow to cool

Once the ice-cream is firm, drizzle some of the raspberry sauce into the freezer-proof container | Crumble the cookies and sprinkle a few of the crumbs over the sauce | Cover with a layer of the just-churned ice cream | Drizzle over more raspberry sauce and sprinkle over more cookie crumbs, then gently stir through to distribute through the ice cream | Repeat to use up all the ingredients | When the ice cream has expanded and frozen through, it's ready to serve

Pictured on pages 220–221

CLEAN SLATE
VANILLA

BANOFFEE WITH
CARAMEL SAUCE

CLASSIC
CHOCOLATE

RASPBERRY RIPPLE
COOKIE CRUMBLE

NEW YORK-STYLE BAKED STRAWBERRY CHEESECAKE

This cheesecake will whisk you away to a decadent holiday in New York! The idea of using tofu may seem a little strange, but trust us, you are going to love this all-plants cheesecake. Try experimenting with different fruit on top too – bananas, raspberries or blueberries would all taste incredible. It will keep in the fridge for 3 to 4 days.

SERVES 10–12

400g cashews
120g light digestive biscuits
120g ginger biscuits
100ml light olive oil
a pinch of salt
300g dairy-free white chocolate
2 lemons
340g silken tofu
300g icing sugar
2 tbsp coconut oil
3 tsp vanilla extract
400g strawberries
50g golden caster sugar

Preheat oven to 180°C | Baking tray on the middle shelf of the oven | Large pan of boiling water on a high heat, optional | Food processor | Base-line a 23cm springform cake tin with parchment paper (don't grease the sides) | Small saucepan | Heatproof bowl | Liquidiser | Pastry brush | Medium saucepan

. . . .

Put the cashews in the pan of hot water and boil for 15 minutes until soft and rehydrated (alternatively, soak them overnight in cold water) | Drain

Put all the biscuits in the food processor and blitz to crumbs | Add the oil and a pinch of salt and pulse to mix | Tip into the lined cake tin and press firmly until well compacted and even | Put in the oven and bake for 15–20 minutes, until firm | Remove and leave to cool for 10 minutes | Lower the oven temperature to 110°C and put the tray back in

Meanwhile, melt the chocolate | Pour 3cm hot water into the small saucepan and bring to the boil | Lower to a simmer | Put the heatproof bowl on top of the pan, ensuring the water doesn't touch the bottom | Break the chocolate into the bowl and leave to melt (alternatively, melt in the microwave in 15-second bursts) | Remove and leave to cool a little | Separate 2 tablespoons of the chocolate from the main batch

Zest the lemons into the liquidiser then cut them in half and squeeze in the juice | Add the main batch of chocolate, the silken tofu, drained cashews, icing sugar, coconut oil and vanilla extract and blend until smooth

Layer up your cheesecake | Lightly brush the biscuit base with the reserved 2 tablespoons of melted chocolate | Pour over the cheesecake mixture and shake gently to level it | Lightly run your finger over the surface to get rid of any bubbles | Put the tin on the hot baking tray and bake for 80–90 minutes, until set but still slightly wobbly in the middle | Remove from the oven and run a thin spatula or knife around the edge to separate the cake from the tin, then leave it to cool to room temperature | Transfer the cheesecake to a plate | Refrigerate

Hull the strawberries and halve or quarter them | Put them into the medium saucepan with the sugar | Put the pan over a medium heat and stir | Macerate for 2–3 minutes so the sugar melts and strawberries soften slightly | Set aside to cool then pile on to the cheesecake | Serve

BANANA CHOCOLATE SWIRL PIE

This dish combines our love of banoffee and cinnamon swirls. We use the same technique to create the swirls in our pancakes on page 273 here, to create a beautifully intricate, concentric circle-covered pie crust, encasing a wonderfully sweet banana and cinnamon filling.

SERVES 10

2 x 400ml tins full-fat coconut milk

350g + 2 tbsp golden caster sugar

3 tbsp dairy-free butter, plus extra
   for greasing

2 x 320g sheets ready-rolled plant-based
   shortcrust pastry

2 tbsp cocoa powder

100g pecans

3–4 large bananas

3 tbsp cornflour

½ tsp ground cinnamon

a pinch of salt

½ tsp vanilla extract

1 tbsp maple syrup

2 tbsp unsweetened plant-based milk

Banoffee Ice Cream (see page 217),
   to serve

Large saucepan | Small pan, optional | Pastry brush | Grease a 23cm pie dish | Parchment paper | Baking beans | Baking tray | Rolling pin or clean, dry wine bottle

....

First make a caramel | Pour the coconut milk and the 350g golden caster sugar into the large saucepan | Put the pan over a high heat and bring to the boil, then reduce to a simmer | Cook for 45–50 minutes, stirring frequently, until the liquid has reduced by half and has thickened to a caramel-like consistency | Set aside

Preheat the oven to 200°C | Put the dairy-free butter into a small dish and melt it in the microwave | Alternatively, melt it in a small pan on a very low heat | Unroll one sheet of the pastry and lightly brush it with 1 tablespoon of the melted butter | Sift over half the cocoa powder and 1 tablespoon of the caster sugar | Roll up the pastry tightly, starting with the longest edge and put the roll in the fridge for 20 minutes to chill | Repeat with the second sheet of pastry

Take one of the pastry rolls out of the fridge and cut it into 1cm-thick slices | Arrange the slices over the bottom and up the sides of the greased pie dish | Use your fingers to push, press and manipulate the slices into the dish so that they come together to form one connected, decorative layer of pastry (you might need to use a few slices from the second roll to completely cover the dish)

Brush the pastry with a very thin layer of melted dairy-free butter | Lay a sheet of parchment paper over the pastry and pour the baking beans into it, smoothing them out evenly so that they completely cover the base | Place the dish in the oven and bake for 15 minutes | Take out of the oven and remove the parchment paper and baking beans | Continue to bake for 10 minutes | Take the dish out of the oven and put it to one side to cool

Spread the pecans out on the baking tray | Put the tray in the oven and bake for 5 minutes | Remove and spread the pecans out on a chopping board | Roughly chop

Peel and slice the bananas and put them in a large mixing bowl
| Add the cornflour, cinnamon, salt, vanilla and chopped pecans and toss until the bananas are well coated | Pour the coconut milk caramel into the bowl and fold everything together so that it is well mixed | Pour the banana mixture into the pie and smooth it out with the back of a wooden spoon

Lay a large square of parchment paper on a clean surface | Take the second pastry roll out of the fridge and cut it into 1cm-thick slices | Arrange the slices on the parchment paper to form a tight, solid circle (not a ring) | Lay another large sheet of parchment over the top | Use the rolling pin to roll the pastry into a 3mm-thick sheet of solid pastry

Peel off the top layer of parchment paper | Roll the pastry on to the rolling pin and lift it over the pie | Lay the pastry over the open pie and remove the remaining sheet of parchment | Press the edges of the pastry together to seal the filling inside the pie | Trim any excess pastry from around the dish with a sharp knife or scissors | Crimp the edges with a fork

Make a glaze | Pour the maple syrup and plant-based milk into a small dish and mix with a fork | Brush the top of the pie with the glaze and put it in the oven for 30–35 minutes, until golden and crisp

Take the pie out of the oven and allow it to cool to room temperature before cutting into slices | Serve with scoops of Banoffee Ice Cream

Pictured on pages 226–227

EMPIRE BISCUITS

We discovered Empire biscuits on a trip to Glasgow and were wowed by their jammy deliciousnessness. If you're feeling fancy, use biscuit cutters to make fun shapes, and experiment with different jam fillings. We've also included a recipe for a simple shortbread. The biscuits and shortbread will keep for a week or so in an airtight container.

MAKES 10

240g dairy-free butter, at room temperature
120g caster sugar
360g plain flour, plus extra for dusting
1½ tsp vanilla extract
6 tbsp raspberry jam
250g icing sugar
3 tbsp warm water

Preheat oven to 200°C | Line 2 baking sheets with parchment paper | Clean work surface dusted liberally with flour | Rolling pin or clean, dry wine bottle | 6.5cm round biscuit cutter | Cooling rack

Put the dairy-free butter and caster sugar into a mixing bowl and beat together with a wooden spoon | Sift the flour into the bowl | Add 1 teaspoon of the vanilla extract and fold everything together until you have a nice soft dough

Tip the dough on to the floured work surface and roll it out to 5mm thick | Cut out as many biscuits as you can | Collect the scraps and re-roll them to use up all the dough | Arrange on the lined baking sheets | Put the sheets in the oven and bake for 12–15 minutes, until the biscuits are turning golden in colour | Take the sheets out of the oven | Transfer the biscuits to a cooling rack and leave to cool to room temperature

Carefully spread ½ teaspoon raspberry jam on to half the biscuits | Sandwich with the remaining biscuits, pressing down gently to glue them together

Make the icing | Put the icing sugar, remaining vanilla extract and warm water into a small bowl and mix until you have a thick icing | Spread an equal amount of icing over each biscuit | Refrigerate for 10 minutes to firm up and serve

SUPER-SIMPLE SHORTBREAD

If you would prefer to make shortbread fingers, follow the recipe for Empire Biscuits to make the dough | Roll it out to 1cm thick, then cut into fingers 7cm long and 2.5cm wide | Gather any scraps and re-roll to make more fingers | Transfer to a lined baking sheet | Gently prick each finger with a fork for decoration and sprinkle with a little caster sugar

Put the baking sheet in the oven for 15–20 minutes, until the shortbread fingers are light golden brown | Remove from the oven and transfer to a cooling rack | Leave to cool before serving

BANANA BREAD BLONDIES

These blondies are freakishly good! Arranging the bananas on top makes them look totally awesome. To speed up the process, use a food processor or stand mixer. The blondies will keep for up to 4 days in an airtight container.

125g almonds
4 bananas – 2 ripe (250g peeled weight) and 2 firm
150g peanut butter
6 tbsp (135g) maple syrup
4 tbsp vegetable oil
90ml unsweetened plant-based milk
1 tbsp vanilla extract
250g plain flour
80g caster sugar
1 tsp baking powder
½ tsp baking soda
¼ tsp sea salt
125g dark chocolate
1 tbsp soft light brown sugar

Preheat oven to 180°C | **Baking tray** | **Line a 20 x 30cm baking tin with parchment paper** | **Small pan and heatproof bowl, optional**

Spread the almonds out over the baking tray, put the tray in the oven and bake the almonds for 8–10 minutes, until deeply golden | Remove and set aside to cool

Put the ripe bananas in a mixing bowl and mash them with a fork | Add 100g of the peanut butter, the maple syrup, vegetable oil, milk and vanilla extract and stir until well combined

Combine the dry ingredients | Pour the flour, caster sugar, baking powder, baking soda and sea salt into a separate mixing bowl and combine with a fork | Tip the dry ingredients into the wet ingredients and fold everything together to combine and form a smooth batter

Break the roasted almonds into small chunks using a pestle and mortar, food processor or the end of a rolling pin | Cut the chocolate into 5mm pieces | Add 100g of the broken almonds and 100g of the chocolate chunks to the bowl and fold them into the batter | Transfer to the baking tin and smooth the top with a spatula or the back of a spoon

Dollop the remaining peanut butter over the top of the cake | Sprinkle the remaining almonds over the top and lightly press them into the batter | Peel the firm bananas, cut them in half lengthways and gently press the slices into the top of the cake, seed side up | Sprinkle the brown sugar over the bananas | Put the tin in the oven and bake for 35 minutes, until golden brown on top

Melt the remaining chocolate | Boil a kettle and pour enough water into a small pan until it's 2cm deep | Place a heatproof bowl over the pan and bring it to the boil, ensuring the bottom of the bowl doesn't touch the water | Reduce to a simmer then break the remaining chocolate into the bowl and leave to melt (alternatively, melt in the microwave in 15-second bursts) | Drizzle the melted chocolate over the cake | Cut into 12 pieces and serve

BAKEWELL TART

We grew up near Bakewell, so their proud creation is close to our hearts. This version tastes incredible, with almond and cherry flavours in every bite. It actually tastes even better the next day. The rhubarb is optional, but we find a little fruit lightly poached in sugar syrup does a great job of adding colour to the plate.

SERVES 8–10

200g ground almonds
200g plain flour
60g golden caster sugar
15g demerara sugar
a pinch of salt
4 tbsp olive oil, plus extra for greasing
4 tbsp unsweetened almond milk
¼ tsp almond extract
icing sugar, for dusting
flaked almonds, for sprinkling
BOSH! Quick Custard (see opposite)
   or dairy-free ice cream (shop-bought
   or see our recipe on page 218), to
   serve, optional
Poached Rhubarb (see opposite),
   to serve, optional

FOR THE COMPOTE
250g cherries
250g raspberries
75g golden caster sugar
½ vanilla pod
1 lemon

FOR THE FRANGIPANE
100g coconut oil
100g golden caster sugar
200g ground almonds
2 tbsp cornflour
150ml unsweetened almond milk
2 tsp vanilla extract
1 tsp almond extract
a pinch of salt

Preheat oven to 170°C | Medium saucepan | Deep 23cm loose-based tart tin, greased with olive oil | Parchment paper | Baking beans | Small pan, optional | Stand mixer or hand-held beaters | Cooling rack

First make the compote | Pit the cherries and put them in the cold saucepan | Add the raspberries and caster sugar | Cut the vanilla pod in half lengthways with a sharp knife, scrape out the seeds and add them to the pan | Zest in the lemon, then cut it in half and squeeze in the juice, catching any pips with your other hand | Put the pan on a medium heat and bring to a simmer | Cook for 14–16 minutes, stirring occasionally, until the mixture is thickened and almost jam-like | Take the pan off the heat and set to one side to cool and thicken

To make the base for the tart, put the ground almonds into a mixing bowl | Stir in the flour, sugars and salt until well mixed | Pour the olive oil, almond milk and almond extract into a measuring jug, stir and then pour the mixture into the bowl | Mix well with a wooden spoon until a dough forms | Put the dough into the centre of the greased tin and use your hands to carefully and firmly press it out to evenly cover the base and up all around the sides of the tin

Lay a piece of parchment paper over the base and pour the baking beans into it to weigh down the pastry as it cooks | Put the tin in the hot oven and bake for 15 minutes | Take the tin out of the oven, remove the parchment paper and baking beans and put the tart back in the oven for a further 6–8 minutes, until the pastry is turning golden | Remove from the oven and set aside to cool to room temperature | Reduce the oven temperature to 160°C

To make the frangipane, first soften the coconut oil by warming it for a few seconds in the microwave, if necessary (or in a small pan on a medium heat) | Spoon the softened coconut oil and sugar into the bowl of the stand mixer and beat for 2 minutes (or use a mixing bowl and beat with hand-held beaters until you have a custard consistency) | Add the ground almonds, cornflour, almond milk, vanilla extract, almond extract and salt and beat for another minute

Spread the thickened compote evenly over the base of the cooled tart | Pour the frangipane mixture over the top of the compote and smooth it out with a spatula or the back of a spoon | Put the tart back in the oven and bake for 40–45 minutes, until the top of the tart is turning golden

Remove the tart from the oven and leave it to stand on a cooling rack for 30 minutes to firm up | Carefully remove the tart from the tin | Serve at room temperature in slices, finished with a dusting of icing sugar and a sprinkling of flaked almonds | Top with BOSH! Quick Custard or dairy-free ice cream and a couple of sticks of Poached Rhubarb, if you like

BOSH! QUICK CUSTARD

MAKES ABOUT 400ml

Small saucepan on a medium heat | **Whisk**

500ml unsweetened almond milk
1 vanilla pod
100g golden caster sugar
2 tbsp cornflour
a very small pinch of ground turmeric

Pour the almond milk into the saucepan and bring to a gentle simmer | Cook for 5 minutes | Cut the vanilla pod in half lengthways with a sharp knife, scrape out the seeds and add them to the saucepan along with the sugar | Whisk everything together with a wooden spoon | Spoon a little of the milk mixture into a small bowl and whisk in the cornflour until completely smooth, then add it back into the pan | Sprinkle in the turmeric and whisk until the custard takes on its colour | Serve hot

POACHED RHUBARB

MAKES ABOUT 500g

Small saucepan on a medium heat

400g fresh rhubarb
250g caster sugar
250ml water

Cut the rhubarb into batons | Pour the sugar and water into the pan and bring to the boil | Carefully add the rhubarb batons to the boiling sugar syrup | Take the pan off the heat and leave the rhubarb to poach for no more than 5 minutes | Carefully remove the rhubarb from the pan and transfer to a plate to serve

Pictured on pages 234–235

MINI BANOFFEE MERINGUES

It's a joyous and magical experience to watch a drizzle of chickpea water turn into a fluffy, sweet meringue mix! Ideally, use a stand mixer with a whisk attachment for this recipe as in our experience hand-whisks don't have the power to get the chickpea water to stiff peaks.

MAKES 18

140ml aquafaba (the drained water from 1 x 400g tin chickpeas)
½ tsp cream of tartar
100g caster sugar
2–3 bananas
25g dark chocolate

FOR THE CARAMEL SAUCE
150g caster sugar
120ml full-fat coconut milk
a pinch of salt
½ tsp dairy-free butter

FOR THE CASHEW CREAM
150g cashews
600ml full-fat coconut milk
2 tbsp icing sugar
1 tsp vanilla extract
½ banana

Stand mixer | Line 3 baking sheets with parchment paper | Preheat oven to 180°C | Frying pan | Small saucepan | Liquidiser

Pour the aquafaba into the mixer | Turn the mixer on to high and leave it running | Add the cream of tartar and continue to beat | After 2 minutes add the caster sugar, one spoonful at a time | Beat on high for 10–15 minutes | It's ready when the aquafaba has magically transformed into a thick, meringue-like mixture that won't fall off a spoon turned upside down

Spoon the meringue mixture on to the lined baking sheets to make nests about 8cm wide, no more than 1.5cm high and smooth on top, leaving 2cm between them | You should end up with about 18 nests (you can draw 8cm circles on the parchment paper, then flip over the paper and use them as templates)

Put the trays in the oven and immediately reduce the heat to 100°C | Bake for 2 hours, then turn off the heat, leave the door closed and let the meringues cool completely, preferably overnight | Cooling the meringues overnight in the oven allows them to set properly and reduces the chances of them cracking due to sudden changes in temperature.

To make the caramel sauce, put the frying pan on a medium heat | Pour in the sugar, 75ml of the coconut milk and the salt | Bring to the boil, whisking continuously | Once the mixture has turned caramel in colour, about 10–15 minutes, remove from the heat | Add the rest of the coconut milk and the dairy-free butter, stir through and transfer to a heatproof bowl

To make the cashew cream, put the small saucepan over a medium heat | Add the nuts and 400ml of the coconut milk | Bring to the boil, then reduce the heat and simmer until most of the coconut milk has evaporated | Transfer to the liquidiser | Add the icing sugar, vanilla and remaining 200ml coconut milk | Add the banana half to the liquidiser | Blend until really smooth

Place your meringue nests on serving plates | Peel 2–3 bananas and cut them into long diagonal slices (the longer they are the more beautiful they will look) | Lay half the slices on top of the meringues | Cover the bananas with dollops of coconut cream | Top with 1 or 2 more banana slices and lashings of caramel sauce | Finely grate over the chocolate and serve

CHOCOLATE MIRROR CAKE

Mirror, mirror on the wall, who's the tastiest of them all? What can we say? This cake is simply stunning. It's decadent, delicious and totally luxurious – a real showstopper. Bake it for a birthday, you'll wow the whole party.

SERVES 12

200g light soft brown sugar
200g golden caster sugar
100g cocoa powder
400g self-raising flour
2 tsp baking powder
¼ tsp salt
4 tsp vanilla extract
2 tsp apple cider vinegar
250ml light olive oil
400ml unsweetened plant-based milk
100ml maple syrup

**FOR THE CHOCOLATE
BUTTERCREAM FILLING**
200g dark chocolate
300g icing sugar
200ml coconut cream
50g cocoa powder
a pinch of salt
1 tbsp unsweetened plant-based milk,
    if needed

FOR THE CHOCOLATE MIRROR GLAZE
5 tsp agar flakes or 1½ tsp agar powder
175ml + 2 tbsp water at room
    temperature
50g dark chocolate
125ml coconut cream
50ml maple syrup
a pinch of sea salt
125g golden caster sugar
50g cocoa powder
2 tsp cornflour
1 tbsp vanilla extract
4–6 tbsp unsweetened plant-based milk,
    optional

Preheat oven to 180°C | Grease and line the bases of 2 x 20cm loose-bottomed cakes tins with parchment paper | Cooling rack | Medium saucepan | Heatproof bowl | Stand mixer or hand-held beaters | Spatula | Small saucepan

First make the cake batter | Measure the sugars, cocoa powder, flour, baking powder and salt into a bowl and mix well | In a separate bowl, combine the vanilla, apple cider vinegar, olive oil, plant-based milk and maple syrup and mix well | Pour the wet ingredients into the dry ingredients and mix thoroughly

Divide the batter between the prepared cake tins | Place the tins in the oven and bake for 30 minutes, until a skewer inserted into the centre of the cakes comes out clean | Set aside for 5 minutes to cool slightly, then remove from the tins and leave to cool completely on the cooling rack

To make the buttercream filling, pour enough water into the saucepan so that it is a quarter full | Place the pan over a medium heat and put the heatproof bowl on top, ensuring the base of the bowl doesn't touch the water | Bring the water to the boil | Meanwhile, chop the chocolate into pieces | Put the chopped chocolate into the bowl and stir regularly until it is completely melted, then carefully remove the bowl and turn off the heat | Set aside to cool slightly, then pour into the stand mixer or into a mixing bowl | Add the icing sugar, coconut cream, cocoa powder and salt | Beat to combine, adding the milk if needed to thin the buttercream to a thick but spreadable consistency

When the cakes are completely cooled, spread one of the cakes with half the buttercream and sandwich the cakes together | Spread the remainder of the buttercream evenly all over the cake, using a spatula to make it as even and smooth as possible | Place in the fridge to chill for several hours

To make the mirror glaze, place the agar in a small saucepan and cover it with the 175ml water | Leave to bloom for 10 minutes | Finely chop the dark chocolate | Place the pan over a medium heat and bring to the boil | Simmer for 5 minutes, until the agar has completely dissolved | Add the coconut cream, maple syrup, salt and sugar to the pan | Stir and simmer for a few more minutes | Add the cocoa powder, stirring constantly to stop the mixture from catching on the bottom | When the cocoa powder has completely dissolved, add the dark chocolate

Put the cornflour into a small cup and add the 2 tablespoons water | Stir to make a slurry | Add this to the chocolate sauce and continue to cook until the mixture comes to a boil and has thickened | Remove from the heat and add the vanilla extract | Strain the mixture through a sieve into a large bowl | Check the consistency and stir in 4–6 tablespoons plant-based milk if the icing is too thick to pour | Set aside to cool, stirring frequently, for 5 minutes, it should be warm to the touch but not set | Pour into a jug

Remove the cake from the fridge and place it on a cooling rack set over a baking tray | Pour the cooled glaze over the cake, rotating the cake to ensure it is evenly covered and working quickly as the glaze will set fast | Pop any bubbles that appear in the glaze with a skewer | Put the cake back in the fridge to set for at least 2 hours or even overnight

Pictured on pages 240–241

LEMON DRIZZLE LOAF CAKE

Lemon drizzle cake is a classic, and this recipe is probably one of the best we've tasted. It's sugary sweet with the incredible tangy lemon drizzle to give it that perfect balance. Make sure to drizzle the sauce all over the cake and not just the middle, to ensure an even, rounded top.

SERVES 10

200g self-raising flour
75g ground almonds
200g golden caster sugar
1 tsp baking powder
a pinch of salt
2–3 lemons
125ml light olive oil
175ml unsweetened plant-based milk

FOR THE DRIZZLE
1 lemon
100g demerara sugar

Preheat oven to 180°C | Line a large 1.3kg loaf tin with parchment paper and grease it with a little oil | Skewer or cocktail stick

First make the cake batter | Tip the self-raising flour, ground almonds, golden caster sugar, baking powder and salt into a bowl | Mix well with a fork

Zest 2 lemons into a separate bowl, then cut them in half and squeeze the juice until you have 50ml (use the third lemon if necessary), catching any pips in your other hand | Add the juice to the bowl along with the olive oil and plant-based milk and stir everything together

Pour the wet ingredients into the dry ingredients and fold everything together until well mixed

Spoon the cake batter into the prepared loaf tin | Put the tin in the oven and bake for 30–35 minutes, until a skewer inserted in the middle comes out clean

While the cake is cooking, make the drizzle | Zest the lemon into a mixing bowl | Cut the lemon in half and squeeze in the juice, catching any pips | Tip the demerara sugar into the bowl and stir it around with a fork until the sugar dissolves

Take the cake out of the oven and poke holes in the top with a skewer or cocktail stick | Pour the lemon sugar mixture over the top of the loaf cake, ensuring an even coverage all the way to the sides | Leave to cool in the tin, then cut into slices and serve

CLASSIC VICTORIA SPONGE

A British classic, this Victoria sponge is everything you could want. Not only does it look beautiful, it tastes even better. With the fluffy sponge and smooth buttercream, we guarantee this is your new favourite cake. This makes a lot of buttercream. It will get messy if you lather it on thickly but that's all part of the fun!

550g plain flour
350g golden caster sugar
2 tsp baking powder
2 tsp bicarbonate of soda
1½ tsp salt
150ml light olive oil
400ml unsweetened plant-based milk
3 tbsp vanilla extract
2 tsp apple cider vinegar
5 tbsp raspberry jam
50g fresh raspberries
icing sugar, to dust

FOR THE VANILLA BUTTERCREAM FILLING
75g dairy-free butter
75g vegetable shortening (such as Trex)
300g icing sugar
2 tsp vanilla paste or extract
a large pinch of salt

Preheat oven to 180°C | Line 2 x 20cm cake tins with parchment paper | Cooling rack | Stand mixer or hand-held beaters

First make your cake batter | Tip the flour, sugar, baking powder, bicarbonate of soda and salt into a bowl and mix well | Pour the oil, milk, vanilla extract and vinegar into a separate bowl and mix together | Pour the wet ingredients into the dry ingredients and mix well

Divide the batter between the two cake tins | Place the tins in the oven and bake for 30–35 minutes, until a skewer inserted into the centre of the cakes comes out clean | Take the tins out of the oven and put them to one side on a cooling rack to cool to room temperature

Now make the buttercream filling | Put the dairy-free butter and vegetable shortening in the mixer or a bowl and beat until smooth | Gradually add the icing sugar while continuing to beat the butter | Once all the icing sugar is mixed in, add the vanilla paste and salt and stir | Put the bowl in the fridge to chill

When you're ready to serve the cake, take the buttercream out of the fridge | Use a knife to level the top of one of the cooled cakes so the other one will sit correctly on it | Place the levelled cake on a serving plate and spread the top with a thick layer of the buttercream | Spoon the jam over the cream | Place the second cake on top and sift over some icing sugar | Decorate with raspberries | Cut into slices and serve

If you're looking to take your dessert game to the next level, these are the recipes for you. You can use our ice cream recipes from pages 216–219 or, of course, you can cheat and use shop-bought. Feel free to pick and choose your toppings too – the candied nuts, chocolate syrup and raspberry syrup will all keep well for a day or so.

KNICKERBOCKER GLORY

MAKES 4

4 x sundae glasses

200g fresh strawberries and raspberries
1 x portion Chocolate Syrup (see page 248)
1 x portion Raspberry Syrup (see page 249)
1 x portion Classic Chocolate Ice Cream (see page 216)
1 x portion Raspberry Ripple Cookie Crumb Ice Cream (see page 218)
1 x portion Soft Whipped Cream (see page 249)
4 plant-based chocolate sandwich cookies
1 x portion Candied Peanuts (see page 248)
1 x 30g bag of plant-based popcorn
4 maraschino cherries
4 dairy-free ice cream wafers

Hull the strawberries and cut them in half | Drop some strawberry halves and whole raspberries into the base of a glass

Drizzle the sides of the glass with Chocolate and Raspberry Syrups

Now add the ice cream | Drop in a scoop each of the Chocolate and Raspberry Ripple Cookie Crumb Ice Creams

Drizzle with more syrup | Spoon some Soft Whipped Cream on top | Repeat to make all the sundaes

Now you can decorate your sundaes | Break the cookies into pieces | Sprinkle the sundaes with the Candied Peanuts, popcorn, cherries and broken cookies | Wedge a wafer into each one and serve

BANANA SPLIT

MAKES 4

4 x serving dishes

200g fresh strawberries and raspberries
4 bananas
1 x portion Banoffee Ice Cream
   (see page 217)
1 x portion Chocolate Syrup (see below)
1 x portion Soft Whipped Cream
   (see opposite)
1 x portion Candied Peanuts (see below)
8 maraschino cherries

First get all your ingredients ready | Hull the strawberries and halve them | Peel the bananas, cut them in half lengthways and lay them in the serving dishes

To assemble your splits, scoop the Banoffee Ice Cream on top of the bananas | Drizzle with Chocolate Syrup | Top with the Soft Whipped Cream, berries, Candied Peanuts and cherries | Give them a final drizzle of Chocolate Syrup and serve

CHOCOLATE SYRUP

MAKES 200ml

Medium saucepan

100ml maple syrup
75ml water
1 tbsp sugar
a pinch of salt
25g cocoa powder
25g dark chocolate
1 tsp vanilla extract

Put the maple syrup, water, sugar and salt into the saucepan and place it over a medium heat | Bring to the boil and cook for 1 minute | Reduce the heat to low, add the cocoa powder and whisk until completely dissolved | Remove from the heat and stir in the chocolate, broken into pieces, and vanilla extract | Leave to cool before using

CANDIED PEANUTS

MAKES ABOUT 200g

Large heavy-based skillet or frying pan on a medium heat | Line a baking sheet with parchment paper

100g golden caster sugar
35ml water
150g unsalted peanuts
a large pinch of coarse sea salt
a pinch of ground cinnamon

Pour the sugar and water into the pan | Cook for a few minutes, stirring frequently, until the liquid seizes, and the sugar crystallises | Lower the heat and quickly stir in the peanuts | Continue to cook until the nuts are golden, stirring constantly and scraping up any syrup collecting in the bottom of the pan to coat the peanuts | Just before they're cooked, sprinkle over the salt and cinnamon and stir them in | Tip the peanuts on to the lined baking sheet and leave to cool completely, then break up any clumps and serve

Pictured on page 246

RASPBERRY SYRUP

MAKES ABOUT 75ml

400g raspberries
100g golden caster sugar

Medium saucepan

Put the raspberries and sugar in the saucepan and place over a medium heat | Bring to the boil and cook for about 10 minutes, until the ingredients have reduced to a thick syrup | Pass through a sieve into a container and set aside to cool to room temperature

SOFT WHIPPED CREAM

MAKES ABOUT 300g

150g cashews
500ml full-fat coconut milk
4 tbsp icing sugar
2 tsp vanilla extract or paste

Medium saucepan | Liquidiser

Place the cashews in the saucepan with 400ml of the coconut milk | Place the pan over a medium heat, bring to the boil and simmer for 15–20 minutes, until most of the coconut milk has evaporated | Transfer to the liquidiser with the rest of the ingredients and blend until smooth | Chill completely before using

YULE LOG

One of Henry's (and his sister, Alice's) favourite dishes from childhood, this is decadent and packed with sweetness – perfect for the festive season! It firms up a little as it cools so make it a day in advance. Upgrade the decoration by shaving over some chocolate with a Microplane or by melting a thin layer of chocolate onto a baking tray, letting it harden and scraping it off. You can also adorn with holly and cranberries.

SERVES 8–10

170ml aquafaba (the drained water from 1–2 x 400g tins chickpeas)

½ tsp cream of tartar

150g light soft brown sugar

50g cocoa powder

100g plain flour

1 tsp bicarbonate of soda

¼ tsp ground cinnamon

¼ tsp salt

2 tsp vanilla extract

1 tsp cider vinegar

75ml light olive oil

unsweetened plant-based milk, for thinning, optional

icing sugar, for dusting

cocoa powder, for dusting

50g dark chocolate, for grating over the top

FOR THE FROSTING

400g dark chocolate

250g icing sugar

400ml coconut cream

100g cocoa powder

a pinch of salt

Preheat oven to 180°C | Grease a 23 x 33cm Swiss roll tin or a 20 x 30cm baking tray with light olive oil, line with parchment paper and grease again | Kettle boiled | Stand mixer or food processor fitted with the whisk or beater attachment | Medium saucepan | Heatproof bowl

Pour the aquafaba into the mixer or food processor and switch it on to high | With the motor running, add the cream of tartar and leave to run for 3 minutes, until the mixture becomes foamy and starts to thicken | Add the soft brown sugar, a tablespoon at a time, waiting for the sugar to be completely incorporated before adding more | Run for 2–3 more minutes then switch off the machine and remove the bowl

In a separate bowl, sift together the cocoa powder, flour, bicarbonate of soda, cinnamon and salt | Stir together to mix thoroughly | In another bowl combine the vanilla extract, cider vinegar and oil | Pour the dry ingredients into the aquafaba mix and gently fold together | Once fully combined, add the wet ingredients and mix well | Thin the mixture with a little milk if necessary | Pour the batter into the prepared tin or baking tray and spread it out evenly with a spatula or the back of a metal spoon

Put the tin in the oven for 20 minutes | Remove and run a knife around the edges of the sponge to loosen it | Leave to cool completely, then transfer to a chopping board | Cut lengthways into 3 rectangles, one slightly thicker than the other, about 8cm, 8cm and 7cm wide

To make the frosting, pour hot water into the saucepan, about 3cm deep and bring to the boil | Reduce to a simmer | Put the heatproof bowl on top, ensuring the water doesn't touch the bottom | Break the chocolate into the bowl and leave to melt | Remove and leave to cool a little | Alternatively, melt the chocolate in the microwave | Add the cooled (but not cold) chocolate to the mixer or food processor, pour in the remaining frosting ingredients and beat to a smooth, thick frosting

Layer the cake slices on top of each other with the smaller one on top | Cut off a quarter of the cake at a 45-degree angle | Separate the slices and place one large slice on a serving board | Lay a large 'branch' piece alongside at an angle | Spread with frosting | Lay the other large slices over the top and spread with frosting | Top with the final, smaller pieces | Cover the whole cake with the remaining frosting and use a fork to create bark patterns | Dust with icing sugar and cocoa powder | Leave to firm up for at least an hour then grate over the chocolate and serve

NOTELLA CHRISTMAS TREE

The perfect Christmas dessert (or indulgent breakfast?), this looks beautiful and is so much fun to make. Store leftover chocolate hazelnut spread in sterilised jars (see page 39). Or double-batch the spread as it will keep in the fridge for up to a month. Add a pinch of cinnamon, nutmeg and ground cloves for extra festive flavour.

SERVES 8–10

2 x 280g sheets ready-rolled plant-based puff pastry
1½ tbsp dairy-free butter
2 tbsp icing sugar

FOR THE CHOCOLATE HAZELNUT SPREAD
200g blanched hazelnuts
½ tsp salt
200g dark chocolate
150ml maple syrup
100ml unsweetened plant-based milk, plus a little more for brushing

Preheat oven to 180°C | Baking tray | Liquidiser | Kettle boiled | Saucepan | Heatproof bowl | Pastry brush | Small pan, optional | Baking sheet | Ruler

- -

Spread the hazelnuts out on the baking tray | Put the tray in the oven for 10 minutes | Transfer the tray to a heatproof surface and let it cool to room temperature

Put the cooled hazelnuts and salt in the liquidiser and blend to a smooth, thick nut butter, scraping down the sides occasionally to make sure it's all incorporated

Melt the chocolate | Pour hot water into the saucepan until it's about 3cm deep and bring to the boil | Reduce the heat to a simmer | Put the heatproof bowl on top of the pan, ensuring the water doesn't touch the bottom | Break the dark chocolate into the bowl and leave it to melt | Remove and leave to cool a little | Alternatively, melt the chocolate in the microwave in 15-second bursts

Pour the melted chocolate, maple syrup and milk into the liquidiser with the hazelnut butter | Blend until you have a really smooth chocolate spread

Roll out 1 sheet of the pastry on its paper over a baking sheet so that the short side is nearest you | Use a ruler to find the centre of the top edge of the pastry, about 12cm in from the corners | Cut the pasty into a tall, narrow triangle, slicing from the top diagonally to the bottom corners so that you're left with the rough shape of a Christmas tree | Peel the excess pastry from the sheet and set it to one side | Repeat with the second sheet of pastry to make 2 tree triangles | Use the scraps of excess pastry to cut out some small festive shapes

Spread a generous layer of the chocolate hazelnut spread over one of the triangles, leaving a 1cm border all the way round. You will only need about half the chocolate mixture; store the rest in the fridge for spreading on toast ☺ | Brush all around the edge of the tree with milk | Pick up the second triangle of pastry and neatly lay it on top of the first tree | Press together the edges of the pastry triangles with your fingers to seal

Now make the branches of your tree | Leaving a 2cm margin in the middle of your tree, cut 8–10 horizontal slits along each side of the tree | Carefully lift one pastry branch and gently twist it to make a spiral | Repeat to twist all the branches

Put the dairy-free butter in a dish in the microwave and blast for a few seconds to melt (or melt in a small pan on a medium heat) | Brush the melted butter all over the tree and any festive shapes | Put the baking sheet in the oven and bake for 20–25 minutes, until golden brown (smaller shapes may take less time so keep an eye on them) | Take the baking sheet out of the oven and let the tree cool to room temperature before moving it

Carefully transfer the tree to a serving board, dust with the icing sugar and serve

Pictured on pages 254–255

BREAKFASTS

Henry's favourite
Baby Croissants

Ian's favourite
Big Breakfast Bagel

BIG BREAKFAST BAGEL

This is a wonderfully indulgent, far healthier version of a fast-food classic. The real heroes are the aubergine bacon and scrambled tofu that work brilliantly in any breakfast-y recipe. The black salt adds an amazing eggy flavour to the scrambled tofu, which has a fantastic creamy texture. If you like things spicy, add half a chopped fresh green chilli.

SERVES 4

4 bagels
a few chives, for garnish
4 slices dairy-free cheese
dairy-free butter, for spreading
tomato ketchup or brown sauce, optional

FOR THE SCRAMBLED TOFU
1 x 280g block firm tofu
2 garlic cloves
3 spring onions
1 x 300g block silken tofu
2½ tbsp dairy-free butter
¼ tsp ground turmeric
1 tsp black pepper
1 tsp *kala namak* (black salt), optional

FOR THE AUBERGINE BACON
2 tbsp olive oil
1½ tbsp maple syrup
1 tbsp soy sauce
1 tsp smoked paprika
½ tsp garlic powder
½ tsp liquid smoke
1 small aubergine

Preheat oven to 160°C | Tofu press or 2 clean tea towels and a weight such as a heavy book | Line a baking tray | Fine grater or Microplane | Food processor | Large frying pan

Press the tofu using a tofu press or place it between two clean tea towels, lay it on a plate and put a weight on top | Leave for 10–15 minutes to drain and firm up before you start cooking

Meanwhile, make the aubergine bacon | Put all the ingredients except for the aubergine into a mixing bowl and mix together with a fork | Cut the stem off the aubergine and slice the flesh lengthways into quarters, then again to make 5mm-thick slices | Add to the marinade and carefully turn to coat | Transfer to the lined baking tray and drizzle over any remaining marinade | Put the tray in the oven and bake for 40 minutes, turning halfway through

Meanwhile, cut the bagels in half | Snip the chives

Now make a start on the scrambled tofu | Peel and grate the garlic | Thinly slice the spring onions | Place the silken tofu in the food processor and blitz to a smooth cream

Put the frying pan over a medium heat | Add the dairy-free butter and melt | Add the sliced spring onions and stir for 3–5 minutes | Add the garlic and stir for 1 minute | Add the turmeric, black pepper and *kala namak* and stir them into the onions

Put the bagels in the toaster to toast

Back to the scrambled tofu | Drain any liquid from the pressed firm tofu | Pour the creamed silken tofu into the frying pan and stir everything together | Once the silken tofu has taken on the colour of the turmeric, crumble the firm tofu into the pan | Fold everything together for 1–2 minutes to completely warm through | Take the pan off the heat

Serve up | Butter the toasted bagels | Put 1 slice of dairy-free cheese on the bottom half of each bagel | Cover the cheese with equal portions of scrambled tofu | Take the baking tray out of the oven and top the scrambled tofu with the aubergine bacon slices | Squeeze over some ketchup or brown sauce, if using | Garnish with the chopped chives | Close the lids of the bagels and serve

BABY CROISSANTS

Henry LOVES chocolate croissants and has been working on a replacement ever since he stopped eating dairy. These are incredibly easy to make since they use shop-bought pastry (we like easy recipes!). They taste great fresh from the oven and are fun to roll up with friends. You can make the almond mix the day before and store it in a covered bowl in the fridge.

ALMOND CROISSANTS

MAKES 12

1 x 320g sheet ready-rolled plant-based puff pastry
50g caster sugar
50ml water
100g ground almonds
75g icing sugar, plus extra for dusting
1 tsp almond extract
4 tbsp flaked almonds

Preheat oven to 200°C | **Line 2 baking sheets with parchment paper** | **Large chopping board that will fit in your fridge** | **Small saucepan** | **Pastry brush**

Unroll the pastry onto the chopping board, keeping it on its paper | Cut into 6 equal rectangles measuring roughly 8 x 18cm by cutting the whole sheet in half widthways and then cutting each half in three lengthways | Cut each rectangle diagonally from corner to corner to create 12 long, thin triangles | Place the chopping board with the pastry in the fridge to chill

Meanwhile, make the syrup | Put the saucepan over a medium heat | Pour in the caster sugar and water and stir constantly until the sugar has dissolved and the liquid starts to bubble gently | Pour the syrup into a bowl and set aside to cool

Tip the ground almonds and icing sugar into a bowl and mix well | Add the almond extract and mix with a fork | Add 2 tablespoons of syrup and stir to make a smooth paste

Remove the chilled pastry from the fridge | Take an even tablespoon of the almond paste out of the bowl and place it at the wide end of one of the pastry triangles | Neatly roll up the pastry all the way to the end, forming a small croissant shape | Press down the edges of the pastry to seal tightly | Repeat to roll all your baby croissants

Place the croissants on the lined baking sheets, making sure they're well spaced out | Brush them all over with the remaining sugar syrup | Sprinkle the flaked almonds over the top | Place the baking sheets in the oven and bake the baby croissants for 20 minutes, until crispy and golden

Take the baking sheets out of the oven | Dust the croissants with a tiny bit of icing sugar, transfer to a plate and serve

CHOCOLATE CROISSANTS

MAKES 12

1 x 320g sheet ready-rolled plant-based
    puff pastry
50g caster sugar
50ml water
100g dark chocolate
3 tbsp icing sugar
2 tbsp cocoa powder

Preheat oven to 200°C | **Line 2 baking sheets with parchment paper** | **Large chopping board that will fit in your fridge** | **Grater** | **Small saucepan** | **Pastry brush**

....

To make chocolate croissants, follow the method for Almond Croissants (opposite) to make the pastry triangles and sugar syrup

Grate the dark chocolate into a mixing bowl and sprinkle over the icing sugar | Stir with a fork to combine and set to one side

Remove the chilled pastry from the fridge | Sprinkle the chocolate and icing sugar mix evenly all over the pastry triangles | Neatly roll all the triangles, from the wide end to the thin end, into baby croissants

Place the croissants on the lined baking sheets, making sure they're well spaced out | Brush them with the sugar syrup and dust over the cocoa powder | Place the baking sheets in the oven and bake for 20 minutes, until crispy and golden

Take the baking sheets out of the oven | Transfer the baby croissants to a plate and serve

Pictured on pages 262–263

NUEVOS RANCHEROS

This is the perfect solution to the problem 'I-want-a-hearty-breakfast-but-also-want-to-be-healthy'. Chock-full of veggies, colour and high in protein, it is hearty and filling. Feel free to have a play with the ingredients – add some mushrooms when you add the onions, or switch the potatoes to sweet potatoes.

SERVES 4

1 x 280g block firm tofu
300g new potatoes
1 red onion
1 green pepper
3 garlic cloves
5 tbsp olive oil
1 tbsp smoked paprika
1 tbsp ground cumin
1 tbsp ground coriander
1 tsp cayenne pepper
2 tsp salt
½ tsp black pepper
4 limes
1 lemon
1 x 400g tin chopped tomatoes
2 tsp chipotle paste (or chilli sauce)
100g kale
1 x 400g tin black beans
16 cherry tomatoes
8 spring onions
1 avocado
10g fresh coriander

Tofu press or 2 clean tea towels and a weight such as a heavy book | Saucepan of boiling water over a high heat | Fine grater or Microplane | Frying pan

....

Press the tofu using a tofu press or place it between two clean tea towels, lay it on a plate and put a weight on top | Leave for at least 30 minutes to drain and firm up before you start cooking

Meanwhile, cut the potatoes into 1cm cubes | Tip them into the pan of boiling water, bring back up to the boil and cook for 5 minutes | Drain through a colander and leave to rest for 5–10 minutes

Meanwhile, peel and finely dice the red onion | Cut the pepper in half, cut out the stem and seeds and chop into 1cm chunks | Peel and grate the garlic cloves

Warm the frying pan over a medium heat and add the oil | Add the cooked potatoes and chopped onions and fry for 5 minutes, stirring continuously | Add the garlic, paprika, cumin, ground coriander, cayenne pepper, salt and pepper, continuing to stir gently | Add the green pepper and stir together well | Crumble in the pressed tofu and fold it into the rest of the ingredients

Cut 2 of the limes and the lemon in half and squeeze the juice into the pan, catching any pips with your other hand | Pour in the chopped tomatoes and chipotle paste and gently fold into the rest of the ingredients | Let everything simmer for 2 minutes

Remove the tough stems from the kale | Shred the leaves and add them to the pan | Drain and rinse the black beans and add them to the pan | Fold everything together and cook for another 5 minutes

Finely chop the tomatoes and spring onions | Halve and carefully stone the avocado by tapping the stone firmly with the heel of a knife so that it lodges in the stone, then twist and remove | Scoop out the flesh with a spoon and cut into thin slices | Cut the remaining limes into wedges | Pull the leaves from the coriander and dispose of the stems

Divide the cooked mixture among serving bowls | Top with the fresh vegetables and herbs | Serve with the lime wedges to squeeze over the top

LUSHY NUT BUTTER

Nothing can replace the taste of home-made nut butters. You can make the process quicker by skipping roasting the nuts, but the flavour will be a little less richly developed, so we recommend you roast them. Keep the butters in sterilised airtight containers – ideally jars with a rubber seal. They will keep in the fridge for up to a month.

MAKES 1 JAR (ABOUT 500g)

500g nuts, we use pecans, almonds
   or peanuts
1–2 tbsp maple syrup
a pinch of salt
coconut oil or olive oil, optional

Preheat oven to 180°C | Baking sheet | Sterilised jar (see page 39) | Liquidiser

Spread the nuts over the baking sheet | Put the sheet in the oven for 10 minutes | Remove and leave to cool to room temperature

Tip the nuts into the liquidiser and blend for 6–12 minutes until smooth, pausing occasionally to scrape down the sides | Add 1 tablespoon of the maple syrup and the salt, put the lid back on and blend for another 10 seconds | If yours doesn't come together into a butter and just looks like blended nuts, add a tiny bit of coconut oil or olive oil to loosen the mix | Taste and add more maple syrup if necessary, blending it in for a few seconds

Spoon into the sterilised jar and put the lid on | Store in the fridge

FRENCH TOAST

This breakfast is indulgent with a capital 'I'. You and your guests will find it hard to believe it isn't filled with butter! As well as the toppings below, try caramelised banana slices with a little cinnamon, or our nutty chocolate spread on page 252. Get ahead by making the batter the day before, keeping it in an airtight container in the fridge.

SERVES 4

60g plain flour
2 tbsp caster sugar
1 tsp ground cinnamon
250ml unsweetened plant-based milk
3 tbsp maple syrup
8 tbsp dairy-free butter
8 slices thick white bread

TOPPINGS FOR PEANUT BUTTER & JAM
4 tbsp peanut butter
4 tbsp raspberry jam
150g fresh raspberries
4 tbsp chopped peanuts

TOPPINGS FOR SUMMER BERRIES
100g fresh strawberries
150g fresh raspberries
100g fresh blueberries
80ml soy cream
4 tbsp maple syrup

Preheat oven to 100°C | Baking tray on the middle shelf of the oven | Large frying pan over a medium heat | Line a plate with kitchen paper

First make the batter for the toasts | Put the flour, sugar and cinnamon into a wide shallow bowl and mix together with a fork or small balloon whisk | Slowly add the plant-based milk, whisking continuously to make a batter | Whisk in the maple syrup

Now cook the bread | Add 1 tablespoon dairy-free butter to the frying pan and let it melt | Lay a slice of bread in the batter then turn it over so the whole slice is well covered | Lay the battered bread on one side of the pan and quickly repeat with a second slice | Fry for 3–5 minutes on each side until the toasts are slightly crispy and golden brown | Transfer to the plate lined with kitchen paper for 30 seconds to soak up the excess fat | Cut each slice in half to form triangles and transfer to the baking tray to keep warm | Repeat to toast all the bread

PBJ FRENCH TOAST

Spread the French Toast triangles with peanut butter and raspberry jam | Sandwich the triangles together, scatter over the raspberries and peanuts and serve

SUMMER BERRY FRENCH TOAST

Scatter the fresh strawberries, raspberries and blueberries over the French Toasts | Drizzle with soy cream and maple syrup and serve

BAKING TRAY BREAKFAST

A one-tray English breakfast that will save you from all that washing up. This recipe is all about ease, so we use shop-bought sausages, but you can also use our BOSH! Bangers on page 95. If you want to be a little more adventurous, add a dollop of hummus with harissa on the plate when you serve.

SERVES 4

8 plant-based sausages
2 tbsp olive oil
1 garlic bulb, optional
4 medium tomatoes
1 red onion
4 portobello mushrooms
a few sprigs fresh rosemary or thyme
200g baby spinach
2 x 400g tins baked beans
4 slices of fresh bread
2 avocados
1 lime, optional
brown sauce or tomato ketchup, to serve
salt and black pepper

Preheat oven to 200°C | Large baking tray | Small ovenproof dish

First get the sausages and veg roasting | Put the sausages, half the olive oil and the garlic, if using, on to the baking tray | Toss and sprinkle over a little salt and pepper

Cut the tomatoes in half | Peel the onion and cut it into 8 wedges | Add the onions to the tin along with the mushrooms, gill sides up, and tomatoes, cut sides up | Drizzle olive oil over everything | Remove the leaves from the herbs by running your thumb and forefinger from the top to the base of the stems (the leaves should easily come away) and sprinkle them over the ingredients | Place the tray in the oven and cook for 25 minutes, to get the sausages really nice and browned, turning them once halfway through

Towards the end of the cooking time, boil a kettle | Put the spinach into a colander over the sink and pour over the boiling water | Add a little cool water so that it's cool enough to touch, then squeeze the leaves to remove excess water | Remove the tray from the oven and nestle the spinach leaves between the other ingredients

Pour the baked beans into the small ovenproof dish and put it in the oven alongside the baking tray | Bake for 5 minutes, until the beans are piping hot

Meanwhile, toast the bread and slice the avocado | Halve and carefully stone the avocados by tapping each stone firmly with the heel of a knife so that it lodges in the stone, then twist and remove | Slice the flesh neatly and transfer to a serving plate | Quarter the lime, if using, and squeeze the juice over the avocado slices

Remove the tray from the oven and divide all the ingredients among plates | Serve with brown sauce or tomato ketchup

CINNAMON SWIRL PANCAKES

These pancakes are an absolute treat. Packed with cinnamon spice and sugary icing goodness, they make for an amazing breakfast or brunch. We dare you to not eat the whole batch by yourself! They're that fantastic. Don't worry if you don't have a proper piping bag. You can cut a hole in the end of a freezer bag and it will work just as well.

MAKES 12 BIG PANCAKES

500g plain flour
2 tbsp baking powder
2 tsp salt
2 tsp vanilla essence
1 litre unsweetened almond milk
dairy-free butter, for frying

FOR THE CINNAMON MIX
120g dairy-free butter
190g light brown sugar
10g ground cinnamon

FOR THE ICING
300g icing sugar
50ml maple syrup, plus more
   for drizzling
40ml water

Preheat oven to 50°C | Small pan, optional | Squeezy bottle or piping bag (or snip off the corner of a freezer bag) | Saucepan | Spatula | Clean tea towel

....

Start by making the pancake batter | Put the flour, baking powder, salt, vanilla essence and almond milk into a bowl and whisk together | Pour into a jug

To make the cinnamon mix, put the butter in the microwave for a few seconds to melt (or melt in a small pan on a medium heat) | Pour the melted butter into a bowl along with the sugar and cinnamon and stir to combine | Leave to cool and then transfer to a squeezy bottle or piping bag

Put the ingredients for the icing into a bowl and beat until smooth

Now cook your pancakes! Place the saucepan on a medium-high heat | Add ½ teaspoon dairy-free butter and allow it to melt | Use a piece of kitchen paper to spread the melted butter around so the pan is fully greased | When the pan is really hot, pour half a cup or a small ladle of pancake mix into the centre | Quickly grab your cinnamon mix and squeeze an even, steady swirl from the centre of the pancake spiralling out to the edge | Cook for about 3–4 minutes, during which time bubbles will appear on the top | Lift up the edge of the pancake with a spatula to check if it's cooked underneath – if it feels dry and looks golden brown, it's ready | Flip and cook the other side for 1 minute, until it is perfectly golden brown

Put the pancake on a plate, cover it with a tea towel and put it in the oven | Repeat to make all the pancakes | Remove from the oven and stack 'em high on a plate | Drizzle artfully with the icing, then pour over lashings of maple syrup and serve

MAPLE & PECAN PASTRIES

Using shop-bought pastry makes these incredibly easy –
just make sure your nuts are chopped really fine for the best
texture. Try experimenting with other nuts for a different
flavour profile. For something a little more festive, you could
also try adding a pinch of ground cloves and ground nutmeg.

MAKES 6

150g pecans
30g dairy-free butter
90g light muscovado sugar
3 tbsp + ¼ tsp maple syrup
½ tsp vanilla extract
¼ tsp salt
1 x 320g sheet ready-rolled plant-based
    puff pastry
1 tsp ground cinnamon
2 tbsp unsweetened plant-based milk,
    plus extra for brushing
50g icing sugar

Preheat oven to 180°C | Line a baking tray | Large baking sheet
| Cooling rack | Pastry brush

Spread the pecans over the lined baking tray | Put the tray in the oven
for 5–6 minutes | Take them out and let them cool

Meanwhile, make the filling for your pastries | Put the dairy-free butter,
light muscovado sugar, 3 tablespoons of the maple syrup, the vanilla
extract and salt into a bowl and beat to a thick cream | Finely chop the
pecans and add them to the bowl | Fold everything together so that you
have a thick, nutty, caramel-coloured filling

Roll out the pastry on to its paper on a large baking sheet | Cut the
pastry in half lengthways to form two rectangles | Cut each rectangle
into 3 equal-sized smaller rectangles

Divide the filling mixture into six | Take one portion of filling and mould it
into a sausage shape | Place it in the middle of a pastry rectangle and fold
the pastry over the filling, crimping the edges with a fork to seal | Repeat
to make all the pastries | Take a sharp knife and make four decorative slits
across the top of each pastry, then brush the tops with the plant-based milk

Put the baking sheet in the oven for 25–30 minutes, or until the pastries
are crispy and golden brown

Meanwhile, make a glaze | Put the ground cinnamon, ¼ teaspoon
maple syrup, milk and icing sugar into a small bowl and mix with a fork

Take the tray out of the oven and transfer the cooked pastries to a
cooling rack | Drizzle over the glaze | Leave to cool to room
temperature before serving

Eat the rainbow

There are so many different opinions about optimum human nutrition. We think writer Michael Pollan nailed it when he said, 'Eat food, not too much, mostly plants'.

Perhaps a less beautiful but more accurate phrase could be 'Eat colourful food, not too much, mostly plants'. It's really important to fill your body with different colours of fruit, veggies and spices.

We're often asked by friends and family, whatever their diet choices, how they can eat more healthily. It's important to state that we're not dieticians or nutritionists, and if you have specific health issues then it's always advisable to see a doctor. But we do spend a lot of time working with and researching food and we believe everyone can be healthier by focusing their diet around more plants, whether you're veggie, vegan or even a meat-eater.

Here are our top tips for staying healthy while eating a plant-based or plant-focused diet.

Aim for 10 fruit and veggies a day
The 10 fruit and veg a day (which used to be 5-a-day) recommended in the UK is a great place to start to ensure you're well on your way to hitting your nutrient goals.

Eat less processed food
The more you can eat food in its original form, the better. Although we love plant-based sausages, for example, they are processed so we don't eat them all the time. If you are eating plants close to their original form, that's a good indicator that the meal is healthy.

Eat lots of dark green
Dark green vegetables like spinach, kale, broccoli, rocket, chard and cavolo nero are high in really important nutrients like iron, magnesium and folate. An easy way to get ahead of the day is to cram loads of these (say 100g) into a morning smoothie (check our meal prep Smoothie on page 206). If you're pressed for time you can easily get green smoothies on the go, although they'll never cram as much in as you would in your own liquidiser at home.

Get lots of colours on your plate
To increase your nutritional intake further, try to vary the colour of the fruit and veg you eat. Different plants contain different phytochemicals and micronutrients, which have different benefits to your body, so mix it up and eat the rainbow.

Make sure you get your plant protein
People always ask us where we get our protein from – and the answer? From plants! Nuts, peanut butter, tofu, beans, peas, chickpeas, seitan, quinoa, tempeh, lentils, seeds, soy milk and oats are all great sources of plant-based protein, and all contain additional nutritional benefits.

Don't forget B12-rich foods
It's great that everyone's talking about B12 – an essential B-vitamin that is present in animal products and which we need to maintain healthy blood and a healthy nervous system. Everyone can be low on B12 (not just veggies). We get ours from B12-fortified plant-based oat milks, nutritional yeast or yeast extracts like Marmite, and we also take a B12-fortified supplement.

Consume a range of vitamins and nutrients
Read up on nutrition and if you're really interested you can include professional monitoring like blood tests into your routine – after all, if you spend money checking the oil in your car, why not do the same for your body? We both take omega 3 and omega 6, which are derived from algae, and occasionally we'll pop a multivitamin. We get our arms into the sun for vitamin D but other than that, we eat lots of colour.

Think 80% healthy and 20% wicked
Our good friend Derek Sarno from Wicked Healthy said it well: 'Eat 80% healthy and 20% wicked and you'll be 100% awesome'. This book may lean slightly the other way, but just make sure you're eating greens and colourful plates most of the time and save the more decadent dishes, like our lasagne, for weekends and special occasions.

Swap to lower-GI carbs
Not all carbs are created equal. We are fine with eating carbohydrates and we're happy that this is a great and balanced way to live. But if you're a bit of a carbo-phobe, try swapping higher-GI, processed and refined carbs for lower-GI, less-processed options. Sweet potatoes are great, as is brown rice and wholewheat pasta. They're higher in fibre, slower for your body to digest, and just generally better for you.

All hail home-cooked food
Comfort and 'junk' food can be part of a healthy diet – especially if you cook them yourself! Dishes like our burgers, party poppers or katsu curry may not be the healthiest, but they're delicious, and if you cook them yourself you know exactly what's gone into them. Plus, they're going to be much healthier than if you bought them in a fast-food joint.

Overall, it's important that we all think about our nutrition and take care of what we put into our bodies. Lots of water, not too much caffeine, not too much alcohol and daily exercise are also important. These rules apply for everyone, whatever you eat.

Gratitude

Ta duckies

You for holding this book in your hands, we are grateful to be a part of your life, even if only for a moment! | Every single member of #teambosh, for sharing, commenting and liking our videos and, most importantly, cooking our food! | Everyone who bought this book and our super-duper-bestselling-award-winning first book | Everyone who follows us on our social media channels – we exist because of you and we are completely, utterly and eternally grateful for you, your time and your attention | You are everything the Universe is doing right now | Go forth, be bold, do amazing things, we love you all

The creative team who spent weeks working on this beautiful book with us | Lizzie Mayson with Stephanie Mcleod for your truly exceptional photography and for making our food and faces look as sleek as possible | Frankie Unsworth for your incredible food styling and skills in the kitchen, as well as Izy Hossack & Hattie Arnold | Sarah Birks for your excellent prop styling and design skills | Saskia Quirke & Belle Jones for making us look super-duper fly | Paul Palmer-Edwards for your design mastery and love of lettering | Emily-Jane Williams for being the best make-up artist we've ever worked with

HQ / HarperCollins for putting this wonderful book together | Lisa Milton for being a total legend and a real champion for women | Rachel Kenny for being a visionary and bringing us into the family | Freddie Kenny for being cute AF | Kate Fox & Laura Herring for helping us turn our culinary creativity into written form, twice! | Also Caroline McArthur & Laura Nickoll | Charlie Redmayne for THOSE Jägerbombs and your belief in us, it means a lot | Sophie Calder for looking after us on the road | Louise McGrory for your excellent eye for design | Georgina Green for your hustle | All the rest of the passionate team including Jo Rose, Celia Lomas, Jess Htay, Jen Callahan-Packer, Hannah Sawyer, JP Hunting, Darren Shoffren, Samantha Luton, Ben

North | All the team at William Morrow – Cassie Jones, Anwesha Basu, Kiara Zauberman & Benjamin Steinberg – for helping us bring our food to a huge and hungry Stateside audience

#Teambosh for helping us create a silly amount of recipes, given away for free on a daily basis, to help us empower the whole world to eat more plants | Cathy, Elsa & Charlie, thank you all for being bloody awesome. BOSH! wouldn't function without your graft | Clare Gray for your dietary expertise and mastery in the kitchen, and for creating wonderful food with us, like the Bakewell Tart and Wild West Wings | Jenna Leiter & Jordan Bourke for helping us refine and perfect our recipes and get them book-ready | EmJ for making our faces look pretty and for your amazing vegan bags | The mighty Bev James and Dave for your inspiration, friendship and guidance | Carver PR, Megan, Jacob, Sarah & the gang for helping us reach the world | Ellie Brown for THAT CamemBOSH! recipe | Alexis Gauthier for the incredible Faux Gras | Rachel Hagreen for helping us find our style | Bodyweight D for the hours on the bars and the mats | Nicola Richman & Sophie Pryn for cooking up a storm with us | Sarah Durber for your friendship and hustle | Jeremy Roberts & team for your guidance | Natalie Maher from Pollitt & partners for your early help and art direction | Charles Lucas for your numerical wizardry | Guy Mottershead for your vision and belief | Amy Gladding for the arsenal of pots and pans!

Supporters, collaborators & co-conspirators

| Damien & Judy @ Vevolution | Robbie, Klaus & Maria @ Plant-Based News | All the Veganuary crew | Anna Jones | Rupy Aujla | Dave & Steve (The Happy Pear) | Si & Dave (The Hairy Bikers) | Yotam Ottolenghi | Prue Leith | Brett Cobley (EpiVegan) | Gary Barlow | Ella Woodward (Deliciously Ella) | Morgan Masters | Ed Winters (Earthling Ed) | James Aspey | Tim Shieff & all the Ethcs crew | Paul Brown & the team at BOL

| JP, Alex, Anna & all the squad at allplants | Grace Regan | Venetia Falconer | All the Vegan Nights crew | The Soho House Group – a good portion of this book was written in your houses | Wilderness festival – you made memories that will never fade | Thanks to all the media, producers & TV execs who have supported us – we couldn't have done this without you | Dawn Carr & the team at PETA | All the lovely people at Mercy4Animals | Rachel Mills for having a good heart | Jamie Bolding & all the team at Jungle Creations for being epic people

Henry's fam | Jane & Mark | Alice & Graham | Bruce | Chris, Paul & Tom Williams | Sukey, Nick, Gus & Arthur | Claire, Nick & Xander | Alison & Curtis | John Dodd, Zoe & Stanley | Davey P

Ian's fam | Mum, Dad, Frances & Stew | Carolyn, Edward & Philip | Robin & Suzie | Simon | Josephine, Katie, Mike & Kev | Steve, Shirley, Lynsey & Kerry

The prosecco club fam & associates (you know who you are) | Alex & Tara | Leanne | Nat, Khairan & Lennox | Marcus, Ellie, Jasper & Caspian | Ekow,

Claire, Hugo & Xander | Zulf, Farhana, Ayza & Ayla | Alex Farbz, Cat, Freddie & Samuel | Addison, Claire & Stanley | Kweku & Angie | Tom, Emilie, Alex & Ruby | Martha, Duncan & Ernie | Josh, Charlotte, Leo & Bump | Tim, Susie & Wren | Nick & Ruth | Maso, Bex & Finn | Tom, Stef & Romy | Chris & Nikita | Luke & Kasia | Nish | Janey | Joe | Jenny | Lee | Louis | Mutty | Louisa | Sal | Tommy | Ben | AK

Our inspiration | Kip Anderson | Ed Winters | Pamela Anderson | Tim Shieff | James Aspey | Naturally Stefanie | Eco-Vegan Gal | Matthew Kenny | Derek & Chad Sarno (Wicked Healthy) | Greg 'The Bodysmith' Smith | Jamie Oliver | Adam Biddle, Joe & the team at GH05T | Matthew Glover & Jane Land | All the restaurateurs, cafe owners and street food traders who are showing the world that plant-based food is awesome | Gary Vaynerchuk | Tim Ferriss | Peter McKinnon | Casey Neistat | Dan Mace | Black Coffee | Jon Hopkins | Photek | Burial | Arctic Monkeys | Tiga & Kölsch | Maya Jane Coles | George Fitzgerald – 'All That Must Be' was the official album playing non-stop during the creation of this book

INDEX

MR. JELLY
and the Pirates

Roger Hargreaves

Original concept by
Roger Hargreaves

Written and illustrated by
Adam Hargreaves

EGMONT

Mr Jelly is the most nervous person you will ever meet. The slightest thing will send him into a panic.

Even the sound of the wind in the trees will make him bolt behind the sofa, quivering and shaking in fear.

So as you can imagine, it takes Mr Jelly a long time to pluck up enough courage to go on holiday.

This year, Mr Jelly went to Seatown.